Confessions of a Public School Teacher

A 35-Year Veteran's Assessment on How
Public Education Can Make the Grade

Michael Marra

DORRANCE
PUBLISHING CO
EST. 1920
PITTSBURGH, PENNSYLVANIA 15238

Dorrance Publishing Co
585 Alpha Drive
Pittsburgh, PA 15238
Visit our website at *www.dorrancebookstore.com*

ISBN: 978-1-6495-7205-9
eISBN: 978-1-6495-7713-9

Of course, for Maria, Matt, Kate, and Andy

Table of Contents

Introduction

"Education then, beyond all other devices of human origin, is the great equalizer of the conditions of men, the balance-wheel of the social machinery."

~ Horace Mann

I vividly recall the moment I decided to write this book. There was no epiphany, nor was there a wrenching story that drove me to move forward. It happened sometime in the spring of 2013 or 2014 when a young teacher, two or three years into his chosen field, stopped by my room to tell me he wouldn't be coming back next year. He was, by all accounts, a teacher who brought passion, knowledge, character and all of those other wonderful qualities that the best educators impart to students each day. He was a rising star and everyone knew it.

My first reaction was disbelief, until he told me about the layoff notice he had received. Per the teacher union contract, his status as one of the newest teachers put him at the top of the layoff list. Last hired, first fired.

Seniority has been an ironclad mandate in teacher union contracts for decades. While its origins and intensions may be admirable—countering age discrimination and the dismissal of veteran teachers who earn higher pay—it has long since morphed into a means of job preservation, regardless of whether teachers perform at a high, medium, or low level of competency.

This teacher standing at my door had performed at a high level since entering our school and showed no signs of letting up. Parents and teachers respected him. Students loved him. But his work at our school would cease because language in the union contract mandated his dismissal in the event of a budget crunch, a drop in enrollment, or a reduction in spending. Like so many others before him, he was being shown the door because of his lack of time in the teaching profession.

This scenario plays out every year, all over the United States, with an astonishing regularity.

I had seen it happen many times before and accepted it as the way we did business. But I was now in my early fifties. I could not turn away and pretend it wasn't happening. In some profound manner my attitude about watching this kind of dismissal happen again without voicing my opinion had ceased. I told myself to start writing and try, in some way, to improve the contract language that hurts our students and diminishes the noble profession of teaching.

Providing a high-quality education should be among the highest priorities of every nation. Superintendents and public school boards labor long and hard to determine how best to allocate their education dollars. But they also hold it within their power to push back against teacher contract language that hinders our best efforts in education. And teachers, too, must stand and be heard over the minority of loud, militant and regressive voices that drown out commonsense change.

Teacher unions have secured an array of impressive working conditions, with salaries and health benefits leading the list. But at some point along the way, we have lost sight of the rights of students, their parents and the taxpaying public. We ignore the rights of these groups—and damage the reputation of teachers—when we dismiss our best teachers while retaining their lower performing colleagues. This must change.

There is a way to address this calamity and make sure our best teachers are in the classroom. School boards must refuse to negotiate contracts that perpetuate the mandates of tenure, seniority and layers upon layers of due process that protect poor-performing teachers. Politicians must be willing to put children and teaching first, ahead of campaign contributions from groups that want this conversation to be silenced. They must be bold and do what is proven and best for student learning. Our pursuit for excellence must be relentless.

Perhaps Russel Hulse, Nobel Prize winner in Physics, explained it best:

Excellence flows from many sources-a freedom of spirit that is open to both the old and the new, an attention to detail that shows respect for the often subtle and complex nature of the world, a willingness to learn and try again, a deep unease with things that are not right or which don't make sense, a capacity for introspection that leads to intellectual honesty with oneself and the world. Perhaps most important, true excellence is never tainted by incivility or arrogance toward others.

The benefits of removing poor-performing teachers and replacing them with our best teachers are difficult to calculate. But this is more doable than most people think, because it is so closely tied to the quality of our education system. Who doesn't want the best teachers for their children and grandchildren?

It is time for this conversation to take place. It must become part of the national conversation on remedies for a broken system.

I hope the reader will forgive me if my approach, at times, is a bit abrupt or not so subtle. This is intentional; I wish to be brief where possible, and pointed when necessary.

To the critics and naysayers, I encourage some reflection about who they would most want teaching their children and grandchildren. I also urge readers to think about some of the wonderful, creative and passionate teachers they have had, and, if the spirit moves them, send a hand-written note of gratitude for helping just a little bit to shape a life.

Michael Marra
Barrington, RI
January 2019

Chapter One
A Confession Worth Admitting

"A hundred years from now it will not matter what my bank account was, the sort of house I lived in, or the kind of car I drove... but the world may be different if I was important in the life of a child."

~ Dr. Forest E. Witcraft

A teacher rarely knows when he or she might have one of those moments they will recall years later as particularly significant in the life of a student. These experiences are usually unplanned, and they can be daunting. Yet they are truly gratifying.

I believe my most important contribution came at a most unexpected time. It wasn't during class. It had nothing to do with classroom teaching or curriculum or anything you might guess.

It happened many years ago on a cold Friday afternoon during the month of February. School had ended and our weeklong winter vacation had just begun. Few people remained in the building. I was wrapping up some work when one of my students walked into my room. We exchanged pleasantries and the student, let's call him John, seemed to be in some kind of distress.

John was a quiet student, not really attached to any particular group of friends, and appeared comfortable alone or with one other student he frequently spent time with. As I continued some organizing at my desk, debating what work I should take home, it became clear that John was not just passing by to say hello. His face was a bit strained and his body language conveyed discomfort. After less than a minute of small talk he calmly informed me that he thought he was going to hurt himself and didn't know what to do.

Few moments in our lives are more significant than one like this. John was absolutely serious and in desperate need of help.

A number of thoughts raced through my mind. In essence, I was trying to contemplate the best move given the severity of the situation. I invited John to sit down and talk. After a couple of minutes, I asked John if I could leave him for a moment and check to see if a counselor might still be in the building. He agreed and promised to stay in my room until I returned.

The halls were virtually empty now. Luckily, one of our kind, smart, and empathetic guidance counselors was still in the building. I quickly briefed her, and she immediately came to my room. What a godsend.

As she talked with John, we learned that this young man was deeply troubled. We went back to the guidance office and contacted John's parents and therapist. Within an hour John was admitted to a local psychiatric hospital for adolescents, where he would spend the entire February vacation.

John successfully emerged from this difficult and trying period. He graduated from college long ago and is a happy, productive adult doing well in his chosen profession. Many years after his high school graduation I received a beautiful note from him, thanking me for being someone he trusted enough to seek out during his dark hour.

When we think of personal successes in teaching, this is not the kind of story we normally conjure up. But I cannot think of anything I have contributed that comes remotely close in importance.

I open with this story not to present my own greatest professional success, but to illustrate for aspiring teachers what teaching can be, and show what it is, in many cases, all about. My message to those aspiring teachers: you will be on the front lines of children's lives on a daily basis. The tone you set as a teacher and a person matters more than you may think. Approachability as a teacher is born from authenticity with your students. Being genuine is of the utmost importance. The trust that grows from this dynamic is bound to create a variety of positive, unexpected developments throughout a teacher's career. On those days when being genuine and approachable seems impossible, cut yourself some slack. There is no perfect. Just keep plugging away.

No doubt there are many other, more educationally relevant stories that have molded my presence in the teaching profession, but John's story stands out as the most fulfilling. Recollections of some interesting classroom routines, intriguing guest speakers and some of the unique field trips I've conducted throughout the years might come off with more flare. But none of those things ever, to my knowledge, helped save a life. So, to all teachers present and future: please keep in mind how important you can be to those entrusted to you. Kids don't miss much. It would be a mistake to assume that course content is the only thing they absorb.

As an aside, while writing this book, I contacted John for his permission to write about this situation. John could not have been more supportive. He indicated how important it is for teachers to be on the lookout and aware of depression among their students. It further pleases me to say that John told me he was employed in his "dream job" and that life was indeed going better than he could ever imagine.

Confession Number One

The story above is a confession all its own. But this one specifically targets aspiring young educators. I confess that while I was in college, as a teacher in training, I never considered the enormous trust and faith that a community places on those it hires to teach its children. Experience and maturity have changed my perspective. Future teachers, please think about this before becoming a teacher.

Chapter Two
Two Essential Elements Every Child Needs

"We ought to esteem it of the greatest importance that the fictions which children first hear should be adapted in the most perfect manner to the promotion of virtue."

~Plato

The hallmark of any sound educational environment is constant attention to that which is best for students. And what is really best for students? We can begin with a few concrete factors.

New buildings, upgraded sports facilities, and other useful renovations can brighten up an average or even a below-average-looking school. Enhancing a school's physical appearance and investing in facilities sends a strong signal to students that people (probably many people) care about them and their surroundings. Their impression, among others, is this: I'm expected to do something. I can do something! Perhaps most enduring for such students is the feeling that they are in a place that believes in them.

Unfortunately, many schools in poverty-ridden areas send students (and teachers) a far different message. Writer Jonathan Kozol describes these schools in his bestselling book, *Savage Inequalities*. Despite local outrage, they continue to operate with leaky roofs, broken windows, and backed-up sewage in bathrooms, along with countless other problems.

What are children and teachers in this kind of environment supposed to think? What type of message is conveyed to students who inhale the stench of undisposed waste and dodge rainwater in their classrooms? Such conditions are unacceptable and must be addressed. But because a portion of the money for public schools comes from local tax collections, children in many poor districts live with this harsh reality, while children in wealthier communities benefit from programs and environments that support student success.

Clean and safe institutions should not be a hope, but rather an everyday reality for all students. This does not have to mean expensive and fancy. But clean and safe is every child's right. Given the reliance on local tax dollars to pay for public schools, poor communities clearly need added help. State and federal dollars must help poorer communities address the inequities faced by inner city and rural school children.

Curriculum is another critical factor in the quest for student success. It lies at the core of a school's intentions for its students, representing the knowledge and skills they are expected to have and the areas in which they should be able to demonstrate proficiency. It also covers the types of courses a school offers and how those courses are organized. Reading, writing and critical thinking combined with analysis, computation and countless other skills must be incorporated into a school's overall curriculum.

Extracurricular offerings also play a critical role, helping to amplify talents that might otherwise go unnoticed. Activities such as sports, robotics, theater, art, music and debate clubs may well be the dominant reason many students remain in school. They also play a key role in helping students to grow and develop. It is difficult to overstate how damaging the absence of extracurricular activities would be to students and a school's environment. At the very least, art and music should be part of the curriculum. To deprive students of these offerings invites them to go elsewhere, if possible. While most parents do not have the luxury of choosing schools for their children, many do believe that charter schools (publicly funded schools that are not subject to the traditional mandates of teachers' unions) provide a sound alternative to traditional public schools.

Beyond the basics of school facilities, curriculum and extracurricular activities, I believe all students must have two essential ingredients in their lives in order to have a genuine chance for academic success.

First and foremost, they need at least one caring adult in their home life who provides consistent love and structure. This care and love must be present at birth and, ideally, continue at least until the child is able to move on to post-secondary schooling. Without this nurturing adult, a child is essentially rudderless in a sea of endless and often dangerous possibilities. Such children are left to fend for themselves and make choices without the benefit of an adult who has knowledge and experience and acts in their best interests. This is not good in any way; nor is this dynamic reserved solely for underprivileged families. Children from all walks of life live with adults who have simply "checked out" from their parenting responsibilities. Children from affluent families can fall into this category of neglect just as children of poverty can. Affluence can have its own ugly outcomes on children, depending on how affluent parents interpret their leadership role.

From the earliest age, parents must communicate with their children, encourage them, and love them. Reading aloud is essential. Studies continue to endorse the multitude of benefits that early education bestows on young children. Having lots of books in the home helps to cultivate a sense of reading as an everyday activity. This creates trust and curiosity along with a vocabulary that will help children become independent learners and intuitive thinkers. Young children who are read to on a regular basis, starting at an early age, are far more likely to incorporate this behavior into their daily repertoire. Parental reinforcement of reading, along with discussions and questions about the themes therein, sends a strong message to children that self-education is within their grasp. Indeed, parents who regularly read and discuss the content of what they've read help children to understand and value this most critical of learning tools. In this kind of environment, the world begins to make sense to children. Curiosity takes hold. And children feel valued.

None of this comes easily when both parents (or a single parent) are also busy with jobs, paying bills, food shopping, attending to doctor's appointments, and the whole array of other household endeavors. It's a constant juggling act that virtually all new parents were never trained for. But there is broad agreement that a caring adult in a home setting is one essential key to a child's desire to be a lifelong learner. It is imperative for mothers, fathers, caretakers, or grandparents to take an honest and daily interest early in each child's life, while nurturing a love of reading, nature, the arts, athletics, and other worthwhile pursuits. If this process is successfully launched, the child is in a dramatically better position to succeed not only in school, but in many other social, economic, and political realms that contribute to their well-being far beyond their school years.

When I think of the most well-adjusted and sound students I've encountered over the years, there are some characteristics that hold true for virtually all of them. I am not talking about "straight A" or Advanced Placement students. Some of them certainly fall into this category, but not all. Contrary to popular belief, there are plenty of children from outside the honors or Advanced Placement ranks who go on to become terrific success stories. I am talking about students who exhibit a quiet air of confidence in their abilities (some not so quiet) while maintaining a genuine respect for the learning process. Most of these students start with a caring, loving and supportive adult early on in life who regularly spent considerable time introducing them to all kinds of literature and thoughtful experiences. Family life takes center stage. Committed parents lead by example and nurture a positive environment based on qualities that include love, respect, sound work ethics, a strong sense of fair play, high expectations and compassion. Actively participating in their children's interests sends a strong message. It can be as basic as making sure family dinners are the norm and not the exception, which allows countless topics and concerns to be discussed and debated.

In essence, a caring parent or parents should have their children as their top priority, which forces many other issues to secondary status.

The challenge in many children's lives occurs when they have no involved, caring adult from birth. Who can step in? How can a child in this home setting overcome the existing family dynamic? The answer lies in coming into contact with a caring adult outside of the immediate family. This happens often enough to show that the possibilities are real, and it can happen in a variety of ways. Perhaps this adult is a caring neighbor or relative who is particularly attuned to a child's difficult circumstances and has the ability to intervene without causing upheaval within the home. Adults who take on these situations can have a profound and life-changing impact on a child. I suspect we can all think of adults who went above and beyond for others, especially children who had little to no control over their challenging environment.

As a teacher in a more affluent, suburban high school, I come across parents and other caring adults who help the peers of their own children in many ways. Some provide rides to and from extracurricular events. Some pay for those events and for equipment other families cannot afford. Some act as a sounding board or confidante to a child in a challenged setting. Having an encouraging, emotionally supportive adult can mean the world to a child. In more extreme cases, a child may need to leave home and reside with an accommodating, empathetic family that offers a place to stay. What a kind, sincere and powerful show of support these adults demonstrate to a child in need.

But I believe there is a second essential element that complements and elevates a child's probability for success in life. We cannot discuss the healthy development of children without talking about their teachers.

In his thoughtfully crafted book *The Education of a Wandering Man*, Louis L'Amour writes: "Education depends on the quality of the teacher, not the site or beauty of the buildings—nor, I might add, does it depend on the winning record of the football team, and I like football." Hence, the most important factor in a child's life during school rests in the quality of his or her teachers.

In *Newsweek*'s stunning March 2010 cover story "We Must Fire Bad Teachers," authors Evan Thomas and Pat Wingert dissect the enormous waste that bad teachers inflict on school systems' resources and the students entrusted to them. "For roughly the last half century, professional educators believed that if they could only find the right pedagogy, the right method of instruction, all would be well. They tried New Math, Open Classrooms, Whole Language—but nothing seemed to achieve significant or lasting improvements. Yet in recent years researchers have discovered something that may seem obvious, but for many reasons was overlooked or denied. What really makes a difference, what matters more than the class size or the textbook, the teaching method or the technology, or even the curriculum, is the quality of the teacher." High-quality teachers are the lifeline of every school. They force students to think in ways they may never have considered. They pose interesting questions and expect thought to drive students' answers. We have all had teachers who had a profound effect on us. Most adults can easily recall who these teachers were, what grades they taught, and why they were special. While I was lucky to have many good teachers, there are a few in particular who made a lasting impression on me.

My fifth-grade teacher at West Barrington Elementary School, Mrs. Jane Kirwin, was the first teacher I vividly recall as exceptional, both in terms of her upbeat, dynamic personality and her honest desire to have every child succeed. Mrs. Kirwin epitomized the caring grade school teacher who expected her students to do their absolute best. She expected much from herself and simply made her model her expectation for all of us. Her smile and wit were sincere and infectious. I'm grateful to Mrs. Kirwin for teaching me to truly care, first and foremost, about the welfare of students I now teach.

I had my next memorable teachers in the seventh grade at Barrington Junior High School—two equally impressive young men by the names of Mike Gabarra and Scott Telford. Both were coaches and former athletes and both took teaching seriously. They each had a good sense of humor, but were not to be underestimated when expecting the best effort from each child. They were popular primarily because they were committed educators who cared deeply about their profession and their students. They also understood the importance of role modeling while doing what they loved. I'm grateful to Mr. Gabarra and Mr. Telford for teaching me the value of knowing my subject matter well, while allowing humor and spirited energy to flow in the classroom.

I appreciated a number of teachers at Barrington High School. Charlie Capizzano was head of the Social Studies department and struck me as a well-educated, caring gentleman and, more importantly, a leader among his fellow teachers. Mr. Capizzano was well-organized, focused, and kind. His classes were a reflection of his qualities. He knew where the lesson would end before it began, because of his organized delivery and laser focus. He gave questions and dialogue in class their due while simultaneously moving the lesson along productively. I thank Mr. Capizzano for teaching me the importance of organization—that without it, little else would make sense to students.

Another high school teacher who impressed me was the late David Battles. Mr. Battles was probably one of the smartest teachers I ever had, college included. He was an English teacher who had a sharp wit and a lightning delivery. His profound knowledge of his subject and uncanny ability to make difficult literature understandable to anyone listening was a show all its own. His background in travel and languages had a profound impact on his teaching style, and he could make immediate links between literature and his students' lives. When you were in David Battles' class you were observing a master at his craft. He was incredibly well-read. It was abundantly clear that this man actively engaged life in and out of the classroom. When he wasn't coaching track after school, he'd be taking a three-hour hike in the woods. I thank Mr. Battles for teaching me to read and appreciate all kinds of literature, along with newspapers, and to vibrantly approach my work to the best of my ability.

At Colby College I was blessed to have two professors who made lasting impressions on me and helped shape my approach to teaching. Richard Moss taught United States history and was one of the most popular teachers on campus. Students from many different majors made it a point to take Professor Moss's famous survey class of United States history. It was a class commonly referred to on campus as "Moss for the Masses" and with good reason. He was gifted at presenting our nation's history in an eloquent, clear, and often humorous manner. He was always thorough and example-oriented, and his dry delivery could be as funny as it was enlightening.

I recall one particular lecture centering on the 1920s and the rising popularity of professional sports in our culture. Dr. Moss alluded to the strong differences that exist between America's great pastime—baseball—and the brutal nature of football. Echoing the comedian George Carlin, Professor Moss noted that baseball really was America's game. In baseball there were "pop flies" and gentle "grounders." Players started at "home" and then rounded the bases all in an effort to return back to home plate. He concluded by asking, "isn't it everyone's goal just to return back home?"

He then juxtaposed this wholesome game of baseball with the raw brutality of football. Football had huge men intent on hurting each other. Football employed the "crack-back block." "Spearing" and "face-masking" were but two names for countless and punishing penalties. Offensive plays in football have names like the "double-reverse" or throwing "a bomb." Dr. Moss concluded his comparison of these sports by reminding us that it was clearly baseball that should remain our national pastime and that "home" really was a place worth seeking and enjoying. By the end of this particular lecture most students walked out of class marveling at how a history professor could hold two hundred of us in such a captivated state. His preparation and delivery were key ingredients to his success. Dr. Moss also cemented for me the strong desire to become a history teacher and to model his teaching qualities.

Barbara Nelson was my Spanish professor during my freshman year at Colby. The sheer level of energy and high competence she brought to the classroom was a worthy lesson all its own. Her preparation for each class filled every minute of time spent on learning and practicing. It was obvious that she had a passion for teaching and came to each class intent on delivering her very best. I struggled a bit to keep up in her class, so she made it a point for us to meet an hour before the 8:00 A.M. start in her office to go over the material in question. Her sincerity and commitment to do her best for each student was an amazing example of what being a teacher should be all about. Professor Nelson was also one of the kindest people I ever met while at Colby.

I hope that all of us have had a variety of high-impact teachers somewhere in our past. They are the kind of people who inevitably cause us to smile when we recall being in their presence. It seems fitting to dwell a bit on the qualities present in respected teachers, so we can answer the question: What are the key elements that make up a quality teacher? I will address this in the chapter that follows.

Here I want to reiterate what I believe are the two imperatives that promote success in our children. Children with at least one devoted, caring, nurturing adult in their lives, combined with committed, effective and talented teachers, stand an enormously better chance of future success than those children who lack in these two crucial areas. Unfortunately, the latter holds true for an alarming number of our nation's children.

Confession Number 2

As the saying goes, words are like arrows. Once they are released, they can never be retrieved. While I do not remember the specific times and situations, I know I have let words go in my classroom that, upon reflection at the end of the day, I wish I had held on to. Perhaps three or four times in my career I have regretted how I handled a challenging situation where my choice of words could and should have been better selected.

Chapter Three

Six Key Qualities of Effective Teachers

"Above all, it is expected, that the Master's attention to the disposition of the Minds and Morals of the Youth, under his charge, will exceed every other care; well considering that, though goodness without knowledge (as it respects others) is weak and feeble; yet knowledge without goodness is dangerous; and that both united form the nobles of character, and lay the surest foundation of usefulness to mankind."

~Samuel Phillips
Phillips Academy 1778

All prospective teachers should be required to read the *The Elements of Teaching*, a compelling book by James M. Banner and Harold C. Cannon. This analysis of the personal qualities of good teachers provides a beacon of guidance for any aspiring educator.

Banner and Cannon assert that "every idea in [their] book rests on [the] conviction that, for those who pursue it seriously, teaching is a calling, a summons from within; that it is among life's noblest and most responsible activities - an activity in which we have all engaged at one time or another as parents, workers, friends, and that those who teach with fullness of heart and complete engagement are entitled to every honor and support that their communities can extend." Furthermore, "while pedagogical expertise and technical knowledge are essential to it, ultimately teaching is a creative act; it makes something fresh from existing knowledge in spontaneous, improvised efforts of mind and spirit, disciplined by education and experience."

Yes, teaching is an art, and not a science, as many of those driven only by data might have us believe. It demands a sound understanding of one's chosen subject, but it also demands much more. Good teaching calls forth qualities that inspire students to engage in the learning process. Each day a teacher opens their classroom door, they hold a front row seat to the human condition. Committed teachers bring many gifts to the classroom and build upon the values and mission of the schools that hire them.

Each teacher has his or her own particular gifts. Some students are attracted to a teacher who is humorous, or energetic, or athletic, or scholarly, or able to sing, dance and play an instrument. A good teacher will reach students in his or her own unique way. As a veteran teacher, I know how wonderful it is to witness the growth that occurs in young teachers who are devoted to their work. So often, they respond well when people validate them and are patient with them. When we think back on our favorite teachers, we may struggle to pinpoint what made them stand out. We know good teaching when it happens, but it can be harder to articulate precisely what impressed us so much. But as we think about these teachers, these gifts from the past, certain professional qualities emerge, and they help us to clarify why we rank them so highly.

Of course, there are many elements that go into quality teaching, but I have chosen to dwell on six that I believe all teachers should possess. They are: Knowledge, Passion, Compassion, Authority, Character and Organization. No two teachers will express these key qualities in the same way. Instead, they display these qualities in their own lives and, in their own unique ways, they bring them to bear in their classrooms. This matters greatly. As we have heard time and again, "Children Learn What They Live." I first read this quote as a young boy while waiting in the office of my kind and compassionate pediatrician, Dr. Lang. It was followed by a variety of examples about how children are nurtured, and the corresponding influences that nurturing will have on their development and view of the world. Role modeling by teachers of these traits is paramount. Teachers must creatively employ them as they face their daily tasks. Let us examine each of these elements.

KNOWLEDGE

There can be little learning where there is only basic knowledge on the part of the teacher. The preparation and countless hours a teacher puts forth in acquiring a true depth of knowledge in their chosen subject will have direct consequences for their students. Students will know soon enough which teachers possess basic, sound, or exceptional knowledge in their content area. A college degree means little if only basic knowledge is acquired. Learning does not stop; for true professionals, it is a constant. There is always new information, and there are new interpretations to consider.

Seeking out and attending professional development opportunities can greatly add to one's knowledge base. And any teacher who is serious about his or her discipline stays current through constant reading, not just in their own specialties, but on a variety of topics. A well-read teacher will have more examples at hand to make their subject matter more relevant to students, and he or she is in a far better position to elevate a classroom discussion through relevant examples that students can relate to.

When discussing government spending in economics class, I explain that our government spends more than it takes in through taxes, tariffs and other income areas. This is commonly referred to as deficit spending. This practice creates debt. As I write this, our national debt stands at just over $27 trillion. That's twenty-seven thousand billion! I ask my students to think about what would happen to their families if they spent $1.25 for every $1.00 generated in income. Their glances back at me tell the story. Then I ask them to contemplate doing this for a couple of decades. Bankruptcy is usually one of the first words I hear, followed by crazy, nonsense, reckless, and so on. With the material now relevant to their own lives, students are in a better position to understand much larger concepts and comparisons.

Effective and creative transfer of one's knowledge to students is an essential part of the art of teaching. I find it necessary to have about 100 to125 books from my personal library in my classroom, next to my desk for immediate access. These books are littered with markers indicating important excerpts with stories and anecdotes that fit well with materials we will inevitably cover during the school year. On average, I will usually read three or four excerpts from various history books during each class to help elevate our understanding of a given topic. The authors range from Howard Zinn to John Meacham, from David McCullough to Doris Kearns Goodwin and Michael Shaara. Providing a wide array of views, particularly in history, invites a fair amount of critical thinking on the part of my students. Transferring the knowledge of celebrated historians to our classroom experience drives new thinking, sparks new ideas and lends much to the broader development of student understanding.

Improving one's knowledge through the acquisition of advanced degrees and additional course work also contributes to a teacher's pedagogical abilities. Learning, exhibited by teachers as an unending discipline, strengthens and enhances the learning environment for students. Of course, this is because the effective and creative transfer of one's knowledge to students is of paramount importance in the art of teaching.

PASSION

Enthusiasm on the part of teachers breeds enthusiasm on the part of students. A teacher's energetic attitude about learning is just as important as a student's own curiosity. In fact, the passionate delivery of daily lessons can mean all the difference in how students view the material and value the course. Students who regularly attend a class where the teacher is a highly motivated learner stand a far greater chance of developing that same attribute. And for students, there is something special about being associated with a class where passion for learning and quality work is modeled and expected of everyone. If we think of the more passionate teachers we have had, how we viewed those classes and how we look back on them today, we know that the teacher's persona and the manner in which they taught was important. This is because passion is at the heart of a quality classroom and teacher.

Energetically prodding students with questions that make them think, such as "How do we know this to be true?" or "Can you support your claim with two different examples?" forces them to consider what valid and invalid comments and conclusions are based upon. A teacher who models thoughtful responses provides a path for students to follow. Teaching the citation of legitimate, fact-based evidence elevates the learning process along with students' critical thinking skills. As Banner and Cannon remind us, "it is a teacher's infectious enthusiasm for learning itself, as much as the student's own curiosity about the teacher's subject, that is apt to captivate a student." I have been blessed in that my enjoyment of different students with diverse interests has, I hope, helped to inform my teaching.

Starting each class with a carefully selected excerpt touching on some aspect of the day's lesson sends students a clear message that the teacher is excited to explore the material at hand. Depending on the subject matter, the teacher may add an appropriate emotional tone that further enhances the power of the selection.

COMPASSION

The word compassion roughly breaks down from its Latin origin to "suffering with." Teachers who seek to better understand their students inevitably have a greater chance of being compassionate educators. While this is not always easy to do, it can pay rich dividends, because it broadens our perspective on where a student may be coming from. When we learn more about who our students are outside of the classroom, we can better address their intellectual and emotional needs within the classroom. This requires us to listen intently and observe acutely. While we can never know all of our students in all of their many realms, we can certainly learn more about them. Some of their qualities will become obvious, while others may remain a mystery. The point is to try to understand how they think and view the world so we may better approach their learning process.

"Compassion requires that teachers put themselves in their students' places. This imaginative act enables teachers to anticipate the difficulties and reactions of their students." Good teachers remember how difficult it can be to learn new material, or large volumes of it. Hence, they "suffer with" their students while finding ways to have students grasp and master challenging lessons.

One life lesson I frequently share with my students helps me to show compassion for what some of them may be going through. It deals with the difference between being alone and being lonely. I tell them that when I was growing up as the youngest of three boys I was constantly on the move. I loved fishing, skiing, biking and countless other activities. Sitting around watching television was not what I wanted to do. And so, when I wanted to do these things when nobody else wanted to, I would simply go by myself. I could fish for hours alone. Skiing alone all day was interesting in that I would constantly meet new people on chairlifts and then decide alone, upon reaching the top, where I wished to ski. Being alone had its advantages. The point I try to make with students is that although we may find ourselves alone (and we all do), that doesn't automatically make us lonely. Being alone and being lonely are not synonymous. It's wonderful to watch students' faces as they quietly grin at the simplicity of something they had never considered, and readily recognize it as the truth. It is satisfying, to say the least, to know that their comfort level with being alone has been elevated.

Ordinarily, the topic of compassion and how students might be compassionate is not part of my lesson plans. But I sometimes let them know that the power to show compassion is rarely far away. For example, one easy way for students to show compassion is to ask a student who may be sitting alone at lunch if he or she would like to join their group sitting nearby. Or they might ask if they could join this student at his or her table. Either way, this at least lets a potentially lonely student know that someone else cared enough to ask. And who knows where the discussion or relationship may go from there?

I told my own three children to do this, and I'm reminded of a story our oldest child, Matt, told me when he was in college. He actually knew the young man that he approached, asking if he'd like some company or wished to join Matt and others at a nearby table. The young man's response was beyond unique. He thanked Matt but declined the offer because he had decided that once a week, he would eat a meal alone and reflect on the plants and animals that may have given their lives so that he might eat. He also said he wanted to think about, and be grateful for, all the people who had cultivated, packaged, shipped, prepared and served his meal. Matt couldn't wait to tell me this. How many of us think about our food, along with other things in our lives, in such an appreciative, thoughtful manner?

One of the most compassionate excerpts I read each year to my classes involves a teacher's admission of favoritism. It's a beautiful story and exudes goodness.

The Teacher

Her name was Mrs. Thompson. And as she stood in front of her fifth-grade class on the very first day of school, she told the children a lie. Like most teachers, she looked at her students and said that she loved them all the same. But that was impossible, because there in the front row, slumped in his seat, was a little boy named Teddy Stoddard.

Mrs. Thompson had watched Teddy the year before and noticed that he didn't play well with other children, that his clothes were messy and that he constantly needed a bath. And Teddy could be unpleasant.

It got to the point where Mrs. Thompson would actually take delight in marking his papers with a broad red pen, making bold X's and then putting a big F at the top of his papers. At the school where Mrs. Thompson taught, she was required to review each child's past records and she put Teddy's off until last.

However, when she reviewed his file, she was in for a surprise. Teddy's first grade teacher wrote, "Teddy is a bright child with a ready laugh, he does his work neatly and has good manners... he is a joy to be around."

His second-grade teacher wrote, "Teddy is an excellent student, well-liked by his classmates, but he has trouble because his mother has a terminal illness and life at home must be a struggle."

His third-grade teacher wrote, "His mother's death has been hard on him. He tries to do his best but his father doesn't show much interest and his home life will soon affect him if some steps aren't taken."

Teddy's fourth-grade teacher wrote, "Teddy is withdrawn and doesn't show much interest in school. He doesn't have many friends and sometimes sleeps in class."

By now Mrs. Thompson realized the problem and she was ashamed of herself. She felt even worse when her students brought her Christmas presents, wrapped in beautiful ribbons and bright paper, except for Teddy's.

His present was clumsily wrapped in the heavy, brown paper that he got from a grocery bag. Mrs. Thompson took pains to open it in the middle of the other presents. Some of the children started to laugh when she found a rhinestone bracelet with some of the stones missing and a bottle that was one quarter full of perfume.

But she stifled the children's laughter when she exclaimed how pretty the bracelet was, putting it on, and dabbing some of the perfume on her wrist.

Teddy Stoddard stayed after school that day just long enough to say, "Mrs. Thompson, today you smelled just like my mom used to."

After the children left, she cried for at least an hour. On that very day, she quit teaching reading, and writing, and arithmetic. Instead, she began to teach children. Mrs. Thompson paid particular attention to Teddy.

As she worked with him, his mind seemed to come alive. The more she encouraged him, the faster he responded. By the end of the year, Teddy had become one of the smartest children in the class and, despite her lie that she would love them all the same, Teddy became one of her "teacher's pets."

A year later she found a note under her door, from Teddy, telling her that she was still the best teacher he ever had in his whole life.

Six years went by before she got another note from Teddy. He then wrote that he had finished high school, third in his class, and she was still the best teacher he had ever had in his whole life.

Four years after that, she got another letter, saying that while things had been tough at times, he'd stayed in school, had stuck with it, and would soon graduate from college with the highest of honors. He assured Mrs. Thompson that she was still the best and favorite teacher he ever had in his whole life.

Then four more years passed and yet another letter came. This time he explained that after he got his bachelor's degree, he decided to go a little further. The letter explained that she was still the best and favorite teacher he ever had. But now his name was a little longer. The letter was signed, Theodore F. Stoddard, M.D.

The story doesn't end there. You see, there was another letter that spring. Teddy said he'd met this girl and was going to be married. He explained that his father had died a couple of years ago and he was wondering if Mrs. Thompson might agree to sit in the place at the wedding that was usually reserved for the mother of the groom.

Of course Mrs. Thompson did. And guess what? She wore the bracelet, the one with several rhinestones missing. And she made sure she was wearing the perfume that Teddy remembered his mother wearing on their last Christmas together.

They hugged each other, and Dr. Stoddard whispered in Mrs. Thompson's ear, "Thank you Mrs. Thompson, for believing in me. Thank you so much for making me feel important and showing me that I could make a difference."

Mrs. Thompson, with tears in her eyes, whispered back. She said, "Teddy, you have it all wrong. You were the one who taught me that I could make a difference. I didn't know how to teach until I met you."

While researching this book, I learned that this is a fictional story, but I find it to be a story worth sharing nonetheless. The author, Elizabeth Silance Ballard, wrote it in 1974. At its core, it is a story about compassion.

Compassion clearly requires us to acknowledge our students' struggles. It means acting as a whole person and not just an educator who imparts significant instruction. Compassion is evident in a steady devotion to each student's future, according to each student's best interests. In the end, a teacher without compassion is not suited for the teaching profession.

AUTHORITY

Without authority, teaching and learning stand little chance of advancing in a productive manner. But a teacher must earn his or her authority. We are talking about an educator who is committed to his or her calling and demonstrates constant respect for students and the learning process. Banner and Cannon assert that "Authority has the unusual quality of being dual, or reciprocal, and thus dependent upon others for its fulfillment; in the classroom, it is composed both of a teacher's knowledge, character, and conduct and of a student's respect given back to the teacher in free acknowledgement of the teacher's greater understanding of the subject at hand and greater ability to convey it. Power, on the other hand, is a coercive force – the exertion of will to command action – whose basis is dependency and often fear. As such, power has no place in teaching; its use is contrary to student's interests." Power, therefore, is not authority.

The foundation of any teacher's authority stems from that teacher's moral, intellectual and professional commitment to his or her students. Teachers who are well-prepared, punctual in their duties, highly knowledgeable in their subject, creative in their delivery of lessons and respectful of the individual student, as well as the class at large, earn their right to authority in the classroom.

Authority also requires teachers to maintain a "climate for serious learning" along with true "mastery of a subject." Sit in a class where a teacher's knowledge and enthusiasm for their subject is infectious and you will find far fewer students doing anything except paying sound attention while contributing to the material at hand.

Unfortunately, some teachers compromise their authority by trying to be "buddies" with students. There must be distance between teacher and student, and a clear line must be maintained. George Washington understood this concept all too well as the Commanding General of America's Revolutionary forces. David McCullough's *1776* describes Washington's philosophy on the importance of maintaining clear distinctions between officers and regular soldiers. McCullough writes:

> He carried himself like a soldier and sat a horse like the perfect Virginia gentleman. It was the look and bearing of a man accustomed to respect and being obeyed. He was not austere. There was no hint of arrogance. 'Amiable' and 'modest' were words frequently used to describe him, and there was a softness in his eyes that people remembered. Yet he had a certain distance in manner that set him off from, or above, others. 'Be easy…but not too familiar,' he advised his officers, 'lest you subject yourself to a want of that respect, which is necessary to support a proper command.'

Our second President, John Adams, started professional life as a school teacher in Worcester, Massachusetts. In his short teaching career, he believed, "a teacher ought to be an encourager…But we must be cautious and sparing of our praise, lest it become too familiar."

Banner and Cannon remind us that "popularity is not authority, nor is teaching a popularity contest." A teacher's legitimate claim to authority evaporates when the relationship between teacher and student is placed on an even par. A healthy, respectful distance allows both parties to better operate in their own spheres, free of crossing lines. Of course, popularity can be beneficial. But if a teacher is deemed popular it should be because of their professional work in the classroom, leading thought-provoking discussions, conveying a genuine sense of empathy for their students and respecting and celebrating differing viewpoints. If they can mix humor into the subject matter, all the better. Smart humor should prevail.

I've also had my fair share of challenging or difficult students over the past thirty-five years of teaching. Based on such cases, we see that authority has a variety of delivery modes. When dealing with a particularly challenging student, one who refuses to cooperate despite multiple attempts to bring him around, I may defer to a bolder approach before removing the student from the classroom. Authority with a flare of wit can often calm and deter future gamesmanship on the part of challenging students. Win the first battle decisively, and you may spare yourself future battles. Under certain circumstances it can be quite effective. While I don't recommend using this approach on a regular basis, it is, without a doubt, highly productive in bringing certain students back to reality. At this point, the entire class is also put on notice that a teacher's goodwill has its limits. A strong message of "play games at your own risk" is delivered to the next would-be disruptor.

CHARACTER

Character and ethics are so closely linked that they are virtually inseparable. Ethics must be at the center of what a teacher does in his or her classroom. As the legendary football coach Vince Lombardi said: "from self-knowledge…we develop character and integrity. And from character and integrity comes leadership." Let us first explore character.

Teachers come from all walks of life. As with all people, their experiences and background have shaped who they are. It would thus be unfair to say there is only one true and tested character that all teachers must possess for success. A teacher who possesses character traits that enhance student learning is a welcome and natural fit. My own experience tells me that certain teachers with limited success still reach some students, while seemingly gifted teachers rarely reach all students. This has as much to do with student character as it does with teacher character. Some personalities simply do not agree with each other.

Often, the degree of success a teacher may enjoy comes down to a teacher's authenticity. Teachers who are comfortable with who they are and who give that persona presence in the classroom send a clear message of acceptance and genuineness. Banner and Cannon tell us that teachers who are authentic "ought to accept their own natural traits and strive to make them work in the classroom for the benefit of their students. Perfection is not required of a teacher, but naturalness is. What teachers bring to their classrooms from their own lives outside is an essential part of themselves that should not be kept from their students if it promotes learning."

Character also involves consistency. Kindness, fairness and good nature are qualities all students expect from their teachers. Consistency in these character traits sets the stage for a stable, relatively predictable environment. Student success is enhanced in a setting where they count on a teacher's benevolent qualities, matched with consistent and productive expectations for themselves. Setting high standards and sticking to them is also part of character development for students. Good teachers know and practice this.

I believe honesty, gratitude, integrity and some good-natured humor round out the elements of character and greatly assist an educator in his or her calling to teach. Teachers must be honest and upfront when mistakes occur. Showing humility by admitting an error is also a powerful way to help students understand that everyone makes mistakes. A teacher who treats an error as a teaching moment is in far better shape than a teacher who attempts to cover one up because of his or her insecurity. Students appreciate honest admission of fault. It's refreshing for them to see adults be upfront and down to earth about errors. It also elevates their trust in the teacher. This reminds us of the importance of authenticity.

In the end, teachers who demonstrate sound character show students how to conduct themselves in whatever situations they confront. They encourage mature consideration of subject matter. They help students to find their way in a world full of myriad options and decisions to make. Students are always watching teachers and assessing their behavior. For any teacher to underestimate this reality would be a gross error. Indeed, teachers are role models and their character is constantly being critiqued. Therefore, a teacher who is mindful of the scrutiny he or she is under is better able to use it to their students' advantage, by remembering that the character they project matters a great deal. Discipline, smart delivery of lessons, kindness, and empathy all contribute significantly to how effective a teacher will be. Yes, character truly matters in a teacher.

Turning to the subject of ethics, let us remember this: teaching demands a responsibility to one's students much like that of a parent to a child. Since times of antiquity, the education of our youth has repeatedly been linked to that of parenthood. The Latin phrase often associated with teachers, "in loco parentis," means "in place of parents." I emphasize that few, if any, professions demand such sincere and careful attention to those young people entrusted to us. With this supreme trust that society places on teachers comes an incredibly high expectation that ethical behavior will be at the forefront of a teacher's character.

A teacher's personal ethics are seen in almost everything he or she does in the classroom. As Banner and Cannon further note, "Teachers are ethical not only because the trusteeship role of instruction requires it; teachers are ethical so that their students can learn how to be ethical, too." Depending on a child's family makeup, teachers may be the single largest influence in a student's life. Sound professional and ethical behavior are imperative in shaping students' perspectives. Whatever is best for the students drives ethical behavior, because ethically driven classrooms have the welfare of the students as their top priority. Modeling respect, sincerity and equity, while maintaining high expectations, demonstrating fair judgment and admitting when we are wrong all send powerful messages to students that ethical behavior is essential to their well-being.

As a teacher, when I say, "I don't know" to my students, there is generally a slight pause. I quickly follow up with, "but let's find out." This honesty calms students' fears about having to "know everything." More importantly, they better understand the value of admitting when we don't know something, as well as the wisdom of seeking out the correct information. Ethics, then, begets ethics. Teaching and learning are united.

ORGANIZATION

An organized classroom that operates in an orderly and predictable manner helps students visualize, on many levels, how to best proceed with their own work. Each day, on the top right portion of my whiteboard, I display a new "Thought of the Day." It's predictable and students like to see what the daily quote will be. Under this quote is our daily classroom agenda, which outlines, in order, what we will be doing that particular day, with homework as the last numbered item. This serves a variety of purposes. First, I don't have to waste precious time answering the "what are we doing today?" question that would inevitably come up. Second, students deserve to know, in some general manner, where the class is heading and what is expected of them. Remember, it is their time too! Third, the agenda helps guide the class along. I look at it frequently, because it acts as a reminder of key items I intend to cover. Finally, with homework clearly listed on the board, no one can claim they didn't know about it. So, an agenda brings immediate order both for students and teachers, while acting as a guide and indicator of material to cover.

An organized classroom is also characterized by clear expectations about behavior. Without a structured learning environment based on civility and respect for everyone in the class, there will be little, if any, quality teaching or learning. So, organization demands discipline—on the part of the teacher, and on the part of the students.

A teacher with little self-discipline is a perpetual disaster. Such teachers send strong signals that they are not in control, and their classrooms accomplish little in the way of learning. A disorderly, undisciplined classroom is ripe for nurturing a careless, purposeless attitude that is not in any child's interest.

In contrast, a well-disciplined classroom can make a world of difference in a child's school experience, and a fair amount of discipline is inherent in an organized classroom. Banner and Cannon remind us that "discipline is therefore the means a teacher must use to impose necessary organization on the potential chaos of all classrooms, and they must do so to create an atmosphere favorable to learning. Discipline takes many forms: schedules, rules of conduct, exemplary behavior, and clear expectations, as well as an equitable system of rewards and penalties." In essence, students need to understand that there are boundaries and know where they lie.

Order and discipline are close allies in a teacher's quest for legitimacy in a classroom. "Order arises from a teacher's leadership, and requires teaching to have direction and momentum." Order, therefore, necessitates that teachers set sound, consistent examples.

Creativity is another key component in an organized classroom. Delivering lessons in a way that allows students to understand their value goes a long way toward fostering meaningful classroom dynamics.

As a history teacher, I try my best to use the material under review to paint vivid pictures of what people faced throughout history. An energetic reading of select excerpts from outstanding authors and historians helps bring the subject alive, as students imagine the setting and elements present at the time. The more relevant the excerpt is to students, the better. For example, when discussing the background of President John Quincy Adams, I find a particular excerpt from McCullough's *John Adams* not only colorful, but relevant to many of the advanced placement students in my class. The scene unfolds when Abigail Adams receives a letter from her sister, Elizabeth. When Elizabeth wrote that "'…as agreeable as John Quincy might be in company, he could be in private conversation 'a little too decisive and tenacious' in his opinions …'" Abigail responded with a strong letter of motherly advice to the young man:

> Watchfulness over yourself was called for, lest his knowledge make him arrogant. If you are conscious to yourself that you possess more knowledge upon some subjects than others of your standing, reflect that you have had greater opportunities of seeing the world, and obtaining a knowledge of mankind than any of your contemporaries. That you have never wanted a book, but it has been supplied to you, that your whole time has been spent in the company of men of literature and science. How unpardonable would it have been in you to have been a blockhead.

Students find it humorous that a mother chastised her son like this, and many also feel a direct connection with this kind of motherly admonishment, whether through their own family communications or through their view of classmates. While reading this passage aloud I notice students looking around the room and nodding to each other about who this character trait might well describe for them at that moment. For teachers, imagining how best to present our subject makes a huge difference in whether our students will take the material seriously. Again, making our material relevant to their lives is of paramount importance.

Collectively, these six qualities make up what I believe to be the key qualities all successful teachers possess. To be sure, there are others. But Knowledge, Passion, Compassion, Authority, Character and Organization stand out as the most essential for daily interactions with school children. These are age-old qualities that have been tested and proven to withstand the changing currents of time and circumstance. I am blessed to work with so many teachers who exude these qualities. It is a real joy to observe these traits when they are put into action by caring, devoted educators.

If we know what qualities in teachers and schools encourage optimal learning, it seems fitting to now address what obstacles lie in the way of reaching that ideal educational setting.

Confession Number Three

I would like to think that prior to becoming a parent I embodied the qualities discussed in this chapter. The truth is I did not. Only after I became a parent did I fully realize the degree to which I lacked some of these crucial qualities. Becoming a parent awakened a far greater sense of responsibility in me. I knew I must view and anticipate my student's needs and challenges as if they truly were my own children.

Chapter Four
Preventable Threats to Our Children's Education

"Yes'n how many times must a man turn his face, and pretend that he just doesn't see?"
~Bob Dylan, "Blowin' in the Wind" (1962)

Before venturing into the troubling topic of teacher contract language and how it can work to the detriment of students, I must acknowledge that it is because of teachers' unions and the contracts they negotiate that we have respectable salaries and benefits for public school teachers in the United States. This is certainly the case in Rhode Island and in neighboring states, and it is a positive and much-needed development.

Unfortunately, these respectable salaries and benefits do not extend to all teachers equally throughout the country. Teacher strikes in 2017 and 2018 revealed woefully inadequate salaries in our nation – pay scales that led many teachers to work one and two additional part-time jobs just to make ends meet. This is a national disgrace.

There is not a sound, competent, well-respected public school teacher in the United States who is overpaid. Quite the contrary. But as public employees, teachers, like other public servants, should not expect to reap generous pay. In most cases, local real estate taxes drive the vast majority of a town or city's revenue, which goes toward paying teachers and other public servants. It's clear that local taxpayers can only afford so much.

Teacher unions have certainly brought pay scales and benefits to a more reasonable level. It took me thirty-one years to make more than $80,000. Now in my thirty-fifth year my salary is just under $90,000. Combine this with sound health-care benefits, and what used to be a generous retirement, and the total compensation package hovers at $105,000 in my district for a teacher on the top pay step (11 years or more). I have no doubt my salary and benefits would be less without a union contract.

Public concern about teachers being overpaid sometimes focuses on reimbursement for time on the job. As the thinking goes, a teacher who works 183 days each year (180 in class and 3 for professional development) and receives top step pay of $85,000 is making $464.48 per day. A non-teacher who works 251 days a year (not including 104 weekend days and 10 vacation days) and receives the same $85,000 per year is making $338.65 per day. So, top step teachers in this equation make $125.83 more per day.

No doubt, teachers have much more time off than people in most professions. The math speaks for itself. How one wishes to interpret this is up to the individual. My question to the person who thinks teachers are overpaid is this: What do you believe is a fair compensation package for a sound, competent, well-respected teacher? Given the impact that such a teacher can have over the course of a career on hundreds upon hundreds of students, I say we should increase the $85,000 per year by 50 percent, to about $125,000. This would encourage more highly motivated, talented people to pursue teaching as a career!

With local taxpayers already heavily burdened, I suspect the federal government will need to trim some existing programs to accommodate for this new financial layout.

What we are talking about here is value. It's about the value society places on those we entrust with our riches and our dearest resource – our children. This is as much philosophical as it is financial. If we care about our children and their education, we should press for the very best that money can buy. Remember, I used a top step salary of $85,000 per year in this example. The Center for Educational Statistics indicates that the average salary for a public school teacher in the US was just over $58,950 for the 2016-2017 school year. Accordingly, if we raise salaries by 50 percent, the average salary for public school teachers would rise to just under $89,000. With 3.2 million public school teachers, that means Congress needs to allocate some $95 billion annually to help make this raise a reality and make teaching a much more sought-after profession. This should attract a greater number of talented people who may have otherwise never considered teaching. Both students and teachers would benefit.

To put this in perspective, the National Education Association reports that for the 2016-2017 school year, the average *starting* teacher salary was $38,617. How attractive can this look to people who wish to enter the profession?

Attached to higher pay, society will demand accountability, and this is fair. Robert Maranto, who holds a chair at the University of Arkansas Department of Educational Reform and serves on the Fayetteville School Board, wrote in his May 22, 2018 commentary "Pay Teachers More - but Make Sure They Earn It": "Teacher pay should be significantly increased only if certification is made significantly more competitive. Schools should be recruiting the most talented college graduates. They also need more power to fire ineffective teachers, just as medical practices and law firms can fire ineffective doctors and lawyers. Teachers unions fear that such a power would be misused by authoritarian principals, and as someone who spends considerable time in schools, I can sympathize. But nearly all principals are former teachers. Recruiting better teachers will result in better principals down the road."

Pay is not the only issue we must confront if we are to improve our public schools.

Beyond union-negotiated salary and benefit packages, there are serious problems in teacher contracts that compromise student learning. Remember, the quality of the teacher determines the quality of the education. We must therefore strive to have the best educators in our classrooms. Three key obstacles—all of them preventable and fixable if we change the language in teacher contracts are: tenure, seniority and due process.

Teacher unions demand that these stipulations be included in their contracts, but in their present forms, they have protected and promoted a disturbing degree of mediocrity among the teaching ranks. This has been going on for decades. To be clear, schools must be designed to foster what is best and healthiest for students. Students must come first. It's difficult to imagine any school or district whose mission statement does not hold these goals to be at the very core of its values and intentions.

The two dominant teacher unions in the country, the American Federation of Teachers (AFT) and the National Education Association (NEA), both use high-minded mottos on the homepages of their websites. The AFT's motto reads: "A Union for Professionals." The NEA's motto reads: "Great Public

Schools for Every Student." While I believe both of these mottos are well-intentioned, each union's demands to include tenure, seniority and an extraordinary level of "due process" in their contracts virtually guarantees that our public schools will never operate at their greatest potential.

Those who disagree with this assessment often think about education from a framework of job security and what is best for teachers. But we must put student learning first and everything else second, third, and so on. Teachers absolutely count, but not at the expense of what is best for students.

As we explore tenure, seniority, and due process, let us keep in mind that change is beginning. Pressure from school boards, superintendents, parents and taxpayer groups is starting to yield results. While this is welcome news, deep resistance from the unions persists.

What is needed is not a total elimination of the concepts of tenure, seniority and due process, but a substantial altering of how they are applied.

Let us discuss each one.

Tenure is an antiquated system that grants effectively untouchable status to educators who have been in the field a specified number of years—in most cases, just three. *The Week*, in its March 11, 2011 article "Taking Aim at Tenure," writes, "Tenure originated in the late 19th century as a means to protect academic freedom in universities. When it first took hold in public schools, at the outset of the 20th century, tenure was supposed to block city administrations from turning school posts into patronage mills where teachers could be fired because they married, got pregnant, or belonged to the wrong political party."

These valid and clearly reasonable intentions have morphed into something wholly different from their original designs. And students, along with taxpayers, have become the biggest losers in this damaging and unfortunate shift. The article further states that "As teachers unions gained momentum and power during the 1940s and '50s, tenure came to mean permanent employment for teachers, regardless of how ineffective they might be." Consequently, tenure illuminates a fundamental disconnect between students and this poor performing segment of teachers. Lifetime tenure granted to new teachers after just three years of service is both illogical and ridiculous. Imagine having a job for life regardless of how you perform. This brings to light the seemingly endless layers of due process that are embedded in teacher contracts.

Due process has made firing poor performing teachers so difficult and expensive that most school districts cannot afford the "hundreds of thousands of dollars needed to wage legal battles against teacher unions that defend blatantly poor performing teachers," wrote Jay Ambrose in his March 2015 commentary piece in *The Providence Journal*, "Across America, Workers Win Rights." The complex level of due process in union contracts puts school boards, superintendents and principals in an expensive and time-consuming dilemma if they choose to remove a poor-performing teacher. Unions somehow believe this is a good thing. *Newsweek* writers Evan Thomas and Pat Wingert state in their bold article from March 15, 2010, "We Must Fire Bad Teachers," that "in no other socially significant profession are the workers so insulated from accountability." They continue:

> The responsibility does not just fall on the unions. Many principals don't even try to weed out their poor performers (or they transfer them to other schools, in what has been uniquely known as the 'dance of lemons'). Year after year, about 99 percent of all teachers in the United States are rated 'satisfactory' by their school systems, and firing a teacher invites a costly court battle with the local union.

With obstacles like this, it is no wonder that principals throw their hands up at the prospects of removing an underperforming teacher. *The Week*'s "Taking Aim at Tenure" article reveals that "In New York, Chicago, and Los Angeles in recent years, fewer than one out of every 1,000 tenured teachers have been successfully fired—and that's usually for serious misconduct, not poor teaching ability." Workers who make cardboard boxes or assemble plastic toys are fired far more frequently for poor performance than teachers who hold a critically important role in our children's development.

My experience has been that teacher evaluations have little impact on who is retained and who is dismissed. Nearly every one of us has had bad teachers who did not deserve another day in the classroom. Some may recall the first time, as students, that they were in the presence of a teacher who wasted their time and everyone else's. This teacher may have been nice, but nice does not equate to quality teaching. This teacher may have been amiable, attempting to make up for what he or she lacked as an educator. This teacher's coverage of the curriculum was most likely general, and lacking any serious level of expertise. Forget meaningful learning or passion and integrity. This teacher probably did a fair amount of grade inflating because that's typically how mediocre and poor teachers survive. They often placate students and parents with artificially high grades to quell complaints. These people are pretenders, period. And just about everyone knows it.

I am reminded of a well-worn phrase used in education over the years. It reads: "If you think education is expensive, try ignorance." This catchy saying is certainly appropriate and contains wisdom. It has been used effectively in teacher contract talks and on teacher strike signs to demand fair compensation for teachers. But a teachers' union that invokes this phrase while protecting and defending poor-performing teachers is hypocritical to say the least. Why would a union representing teachers fight to protect and defend incompetent and uninspired teachers? The short answer is that unions have some historically bad habits that they refuse to relinquish. Fresh thinking and open-minded leadership are long overdue.

Antonio Villaraigosa, the former mayor of Los Angeles, former speaker of the California State Assembly, and a former organizer with United Teachers of Los Angeles, offers a voice of clarity when he says: "We need to identify the small percentage who lack the passion or capacity to teach and counsel them out of the field. That's not an indictment of the teaching profession, nor is it anti-union. It's a fact of life in every field. Countless teachers and union leaders agree with these commonsense measures, yet at their conventions, the most regressive voices are amplified while the reasonable, fair-minded voices aren't heard."

Aggressive, adversarial union members must stop proclaiming they put kids first when the facts prove otherwise.

I maintain that firing bad teachers is a must. *Newsweek* said it best when it ran a bold and searing cover page for its March 15, 2010 issue. It ran with the title:

The Key to Saving American Education

We must fire bad teachers
We must fire bad teachers
We must fire bad teachers
We must fire bad teachers

We must fire bad teachers
We must fire bad teachers
We must fire bad teachers
We must fire bad teachers
We must fire bad teachers
We must fire bad teachers

Seeking to eliminate poor-performing teachers is almost always twisted by union rhetoric to be anti-teacher. This is simply not true. Society admires and respects good teaching. Opposing the elimination of poor-performing teachers is like saying the removal of an incompetent doctor is anti-doctor or anti-medicine. This is misguided thinking at best. But the tremendous costs of firing bad teachers are real. Ambrose writes that "Joel Klein, former chancellor of New York City schools, has emboldened the anti-union argument with specifics about how it can take as much as two years and cost more than $300,000 to get an incompetent teacher out of the classroom in the city. That is an anti-student abomination." Union officials at the national, state and sometimes local level become irate at the suggestion that unions get in the way of providing the best education for our children. Yet having the best teachers in the classroom goes a long way toward achieving that. And protecting poor-performing teachers means that better teachers will not be in the classroom. Why would we ever put the interests of adults above those of students in our schools?

Teacher unions claim tenure and seniority protect their members against arbitrary firings. This claim has some merit. Teachers deserve due process and the right to defend themselves. But protecting teachers against arbitrary dismissals and guaranteeing due process should not result in legitimate dismissals taking several years and costing hundreds of thousands of dollars. Unions look foolish when they defend blatantly bad teachers. How could this ever be in the union's best interests, or that of countless good and excellent teachers? In my experience, the vast majority of teachers are appalled when ineffective teachers are kept among their ranks. And don't believe teachers don't know who's who in the teacher quality pecking order.

The bottom line: the process for removing a poor performing teacher should be fair. But it should be far more expedient than current practice dictates. Unions and school boards must make changes in this area—which would serve the interests of both—a top priority.

This is not to say that tenure is without any positive aspects. It certainly allows teachers to speak out openly and honestly without fear of reprisal or dismissal. Teachers should be part of any conversation regarding what goes on in their district and schools. School committees and administrators often decide to eliminate certain programs or cut back supporting resources. Are teachers to remain silent when they understand the negative impact of such decisions? Should teachers be silent when they have overcrowded classrooms or woefully inadequate materials? If a teacher is the only advocate a student might have, is he or she supposed to keep quiet and watch from the sidelines as a struggling student drops out? Solving a challenging situation may call for a bold approach or intervention. Tenure allows that teacher to speak openly and yes, boldly.

School committees that regularly hear from concerned teachers who are honest enough to voice their opposition to proposed changes are at least able to consider a different perspective. Tenure may well keep healthy debate alive in a school system. In too many school systems we see school board members elected for one specific reason, to cut costs. But quality programs that impact students are best understood by the teachers involved. Thus, they must be able to speak out and defend what is in their students' best interests, without the threat of losing their jobs. Sometimes the conversation gets heated. But this is all the more reason to have a passionate teacher who is unafraid to speak his or her mind.

Another argument for tenure is that without it a school district may choose to lay off talented veteran teachers earning the highest salaries, simply to cut costs. Without the protection tenure guarantees, the temptation to replace these veteran educators will prove irresistible to many school boards. With quality out and costs lowered, a school board could quickly dismantle what was once a high-functioning education program. This unfortunate development would be in nobody's best interest. So, tenure does have its merits. But not when it is so cumbersome that it gets in the way of decisions that are in the best interests of students.

Seniority runs along the same lines as tenure. And like tenure, seniority exists for the benefit of the teachers in the system, not for the benefit of our students. Under union contract rules, teachers who have the most years in a system receive the highest salaries. The longer a teacher remains in a system, the higher the salary, until it caps out at the top level, usually after ten to twelve years.

Seniority often dictates layoff policy. "In almost every state across the country, the 'last in, first out' policy is softening America's competitive edge," says Michelle Rhee, former schools chancellor of Washington, DC. The reason: "We end up firing some of our most highly effective teachers."

Teacher accountability lies at the very core of the issue. Why would we ever lay off a highly effective, less-senior teacher, and keep a lower-performing teacher with more seniority? Again, many who raise the issue of teacher quality are labeled as anti-teacher or teacher-bashers. Yet what other professions operate on such feeble expectations from their corps of professionals? What other profession has few, if any, consequences for poor performance? I believe that tenure and seniority absolutely protect and promote poor-performing teachers. Do we really believe a system that has no rewards for excellence will attract highly motivated professionals who will make exactly the same amount of money as poor performers? Where is the logic here? And where is the outrage?

Creative alternatives other than the total elimination of tenure and seniority as we know them will be discussed later in this book. Teacher union resistance is virtually guaranteed. But the argument for keeping tenure, seniority and due process in their current forms is mere fiction masquerading as deep necessity.

And masquerade it does. The August/September 2010 issue of the National Education Association's *NEA Today*—the national publication for members of the largest teacher union in the United States—had a picture of a young female teacher on the cover with the title "What Now?" Underneath, the subtitle read: "This Teacher of the Year was laid off, but her students still need her. When will public officials stand up for education?" I read this story with great interest. Why would a local public school system lay off its Teacher of the Year?

As I studied this article it became glaringly apparent how distorted the NEA can be. By all accounts, this inspiring young educator should have been one of the last to lose her job in a layoff situation, certainly not one of the first.

But the seniority demanded in her contract, by her own union, mandated that she be laid off. In fact, I phoned the NEA national headquarters and left a message, asking if the teacher's layoff was due to seniority. A day later I received a phone message indicating that this was the reason. The very union that placed her on its cover page and portrayed her as a pawn at the mercy of her municipality guaranteed, through its own senseless contract demands, that she would be among the first to be laid off. She had no one to blame but her own union, which collected dues from her paychecks while she was employed. And for what? Presumably to assist her in labor issues?

The union could have preserved this rising star by supporting layoff policies that are based on teacher quality, but instead it stuck to its archaic, anti-student policy of "last in, first out." Randi Weingarten, president of the American Federation of Teachers, the second largest teachers' union in the US, defends this senseless policy, saying "that in tough economic times... the people who have experience are not the first to be let go." Conceptually this point has some merit. But in reality, poor performing senior teachers prove this thinking dreadfully wrong. Ms. Weingarten's skewed assumption here is that seniority is the ultimate indicator of teacher quality. But what this actually does is put adults before students in education. Obviously, this is not in the nation's best interest. We must stop protecting ineffective teachers. We must stop laying off high-quality teachers who lack seniority. Have the teachers' unions become blind to their own blindness on this crucial matter?

Public education is just that, public. There are finite resources, and political factions are constantly debating on how to spend tax dollars. That is the way of democracy. With unavoidable limits on public dollars, we all understand budgets will be at the whim, more or less, of residents and their elected officials. Yet this is not how the article in *NEA Today* portrayed the young teacher's layoff. Instead, the article blamed only elected officials. A bold print sentence at the beginning of the article stated: "Keeping great educators in our schools isn't made easier when elected officials write off public education during a funding crisis." This self-serving and evasive rhetoric is damaging, and it hurts children the most. It should be an embarrassment for unions, but somehow it is not. I wonder if anyone within the NEA had the courtesy to remind the teacher that it was demands by the NEA in her contract that guaranteed her layoff?

With such shortsighted leadership, it is no wonder that teacher unions are finally under pressure. The court of public opinion demands that we place, and retain, the highest-qualified teachers in our classrooms.

If we look at the power and influence a high quality teacher has in stimulating academic success, we may begin to appreciate this teacher all the more. Let's say students in this teacher's class meet once a day for an hour. Over the course of a year they are influenced by this teacher for 180 hours. Thinking cumulatively helps to quantify how important it is to have the best teachers in our classrooms. Students under their supervision and direction receive high performance teaching on a daily basis. The curriculum comes alive. Students are challenged to critically analyze and objectively assess the subject matter. Kati Haycock of The Education Trust states in Thomas and Wingert's article that "kids who have two, three, four strong teachers in a row will eventually excel, no matter what their background, while kids who have even two weak teachers in a row will never recover."

The point is that the classroom is a place that kids will remember for a long time. Ideally, it will be where they learned and laughed. It will be where they were encouraged to reflect, exchange opinions, think for themselves, test their ideas, and much more. Yet because of contract language that most students know little about, a quality teacher can be replaced by another teacher who has simply been in the system longer. And if this replacement teacher is mediocre or poor, it will be downright depressing to calculate the true loss of our less senior, high-octane teacher. Students may now face 180 hours of basic, uninspired teaching from a senior teacher – someone who should have been dismissed many years ago. It's tough to calculate the damage. How can we let this continue?

Ask principals and superintendents if they would prefer the option of annually replacing the bottom 5 to 10 percent of their teachers and you will immediately see smiles on their faces. But their look will quickly fade as they calculate the history of such a question. Tenure, seniority and a staggering level of due process haven't allowed this to happen. I have seen this process play out too many times over my three-plus decades of teaching. It never works in favor of the kids. Occasionally, even the teacher replacing a non-tenured teacher has the decency to admit the flawed outcome. I remember one particular instance when this honest admission by a "senior" teacher caught me by surprise. It was refreshing on a number of levels. To the best of my recollection, the story unfolded as follows:

Many years ago, my school had a rising star among our newer teachers. This newer teacher was as solid and committed an educator as many true and tested top veterans. He was well-read, loved his subject, committed to his students and firing on all cylinders. He set high expectations for his students and did everything in his power to help them succeed. He arrived an hour before school began and regularly stayed well after any bells had ended the day. His classes were well-organized, focused and student-centered, with a continuum of smart questions flowing to keep all students on their toes. He also offered his services on committees, shared materials with colleagues and was fun to be around. Every school would have been blessed to have him. Loved by his students and respected by all, this teacher was a real asset.

Unfortunately, but quite predictably, he was dismissed during his second year — "bumped" by a more senior teacher whose position was eliminated at another school. This other teacher had a couple of years on the newer teacher and was entitled to the less senior teacher's position. Without any consideration for teacher quality or what would be best for the students, our newer teacher was out and a clearly inferior teacher replaced him. Everyone knew it, and the senior teacher even admitted it.

Regrettably, this scene has played out thousands of times over the last six or so decades because of the seniority language demanded in union contracts. Imagine how many wonderful teachers have been driven from education because of pernicious and regressive policies like this. In their place, districts retained lackluster teachers for decades because they had tenure and seniority. What an unmitigated disaster for our children, parents, local taxpayers and the nation at large.

If unions are serious about providing the best education for our children, as so many of their slogans indicate, then they must adjust the elements of tenure, seniority and due process in their contracts to make what is best for students their guiding focus. Only then will students and taxpayers, along with the teaching profession, receive the benefits and respect they truly deserve.

Confession Number Four

A teacher must always be careful about judging his or her students. We often know so little about them other than what we observe in the short time we are together in class.

I was reminded of this when observing Unified sports, a program that affords our special needs students the opportunity to play basketball, volleyball and other team sports against Unified teams from other schools. It's a superb way to encourage many children who would otherwise be excluded from playing team sports to play on a team of their own. During games and practices a couple of students from the general population volunteer and help keep the games and practices moving along and make sure everyone gets an opportunity to play. What a wonderful program.

So, here is my confession. I haven't attended anywhere near enough of these worthwhile happenings during my career. These spirited events make up the soul of what a school is all about. They showcase wonderful kids playing for the sake of fun and compassion. I urge teachers to make time to attend such important events. Everyone attending is better for it.

Chapter Five
Newspaper Commentary

"Change is the end result of all true learning."
~Leo Buscaglia

This chapter brings together a couple of opinion articles that appeared in the *Providence Journal* in 2018. To spare the reader, I have omitted two commentaries that I wrote dwelling on much of what chapter four just covered. The two commentaries here provide a small window into the differing thoughts regarding teacher tenure, seniority and the astonishing level of due process that protects ill-equipped and under-performing teachers.

The first writer is Erika Sanzi of Cumberland, Rhode Island. *The Providence Journal* indicates that she is an occasional contributor and writes for *Education Post* and Goodschoolhunting.org. She is a senior visiting fellow at the Fordham Institute.

The second commentary was written by Francis Flynn, president of the Rhode Island Federation of Teachers and Health Professionals. The title of his commentary, "No Need to Change Teacher Seniority," says it all.

Below, Ms. Sanzi's commentary was printed July 1,2018. She is, by all counts, a sound steward of the public good.

Teachers Unions Need to Change

Some politicians were screaming from the rooftops about the unfairness of last week's Janus ruling by the Supreme Court. But in their passion-filled proclamations about the destruction of the middle class, almost no one talked about what's best for public school students, often taught by unionized teachers. If the well-being of children—who are mandated by law to attend school—isn't front and center, I don't want to hear the wailing.

The Supreme Court was asked to consider whether collective bargaining is inherently political. Any honest person knows that it is. And that is why the justices voted 5-4 to say that it violates workers' rights to compel them to pay union fees against their will.

Decisions about budgets, contracts, teacher placements, tenure rules, seniority and pensions are purely political because they speak to our values, priorities and beliefs about how best to be good stewards of public dollars when it comes to educating children. When half the high schools in America don't offer calculus and the average counselor has a caseload of 482 students, we can't pretend that equity and opportunity aren't stuck in the clutches of an ugly fight about where dollars should be spent.

And because of inflexible and irresponsible collective bargaining agreements—many from decades ago—and resulting contractual obligations, superintendents in cash-strapped districts find that more than 95 percent of their money is spoken for before they buy one book or add one class.

My lens on this long-awaited decision is a bit unique. I was a member of two teachers' unions and also served on an elected school committee.

One of the unions I was in did performance-driven layoffs. If more unions operated that way, perhaps my pom-poms to celebrate the Janus ruling wouldn't be quite so big. But in the second union to which I was obligated to pay dues—the one that sent me a never-ending stream of high gloss "Vote for Howard Dean" mailers until that fateful scream—personnel decisions were governed by a "last in, first out" policy that sent the recent hires packing even in cases where they were the best teacher in their department. Because it wasn't about kids, period.

During my two-year term on an elected school committee, I felt something close to trauma when I witnessed the behavior of union lawyers who, in their quest to protect teachers who were literally damaging kids, would say and do the most despicable things I had ever seen in a room full of adults. They would lie, insult and bully just to secure benefits for their members that they knew would be detrimental for students. I felt physically sick during and after meetings. I will never un-see what I saw during that time.

Public sector unions could have avoided this outcome easily. Rather than double down in their fights against parents who are distraught over the kinds of people the unions protect and force their children to spend their days with, they could have been honest about what was happening in those classrooms and taken action to protect children.

They could have spoken up about low-income children most often finding themselves in classrooms with the least experienced teachers. They could have admitted that laying off the best educators because of arcane seniority rules is wrong and pushed for reforms that would let the best teachers remain with children who need them. And they could have admitted that one size doesn't fit all – that parents, rich or poor, should be empowered to choose the school that best fits their child's needs.

They chose to do none of those things. Now they have a chance to change course.

In response to my June 10 commentary (contents outlined in previous chapter), Francis Flynn, the president of the Rhode Island Federation of Teachers and Healthcare Professionals, wrote the following, which was printed on July 2, 2018.

No Need to Change Teacher Seniority

In his June 10 Commentary piece ("Uninspired Teachers Hurt R.I. Students"), Portsmouth teacher Michael Marra criticized the effects of teacher tenure and seniority. As president of the Rhode Island Federation of Teachers, I find that Mr. Marra's remarks are uninformed and misdirected.

Rhode Island General Law $16-2-11 confers on the superintendent of each school district the "care and supervision of public schools" and "the appointment of employees of the district." In fact, no teachers' union official in Rhode Island has ever had the authority to hire or terminate a single teacher.

Teacher tenure laws were first adopted in Rhode Island in 1946 and teachers' ability to enforce due process rights were further strengthened by the 1966 passage of the Michaelson Act, granting teachers the right to organize. Prior to that there was little protection from discrimination or a teacher's right to free speech and association, which are protected by the US Constitution. Employment decisions were highly capricious and arbitrary. Many may recall that even pregnancy was used as a legitimate reason to terminate a teacher. Eliminating tenure and seniority would open the door to nepotism, ageism, sexism, racism, favoritism, and any other highly subjective employment practice.

Having taught for twenty-one years (sic), Mr. Marra is surely quite aware that collective bargaining involves mutual consent from both parties. Our local unions abide by a democratic process. I have been an educator for more than forty years, including thirty-four years as a public school teacher and most recently as a state union president. Throughout that time, I have been involved in numerous contract negotiations, during which we have always solicited the suggestions of our members when formulating and prioritizing proposals. All contract settlements are subject to ratification by the members. Never once has anyone suggested that we eliminate teacher tenure or seniority.

Much of Mr. Marra's complaint deals with due process rights granted to individual teachers by Rhode Island General Law 616-13-1-8. The Rhode Island Supreme Court considers teacher tenure a "constitutionally protected property interest" and a tenured teacher cannot be terminated without "good or just cause." Those due process rights also compel the union to provide representation through that process or risk facing legal consequences. Such due process exists in every union contract and is not unique to teachers.

While Mr. Marra and I may disagree on the method to arrive there, we are in full agreement that we need to have a qualified, motivated, appropriately certified teacher in every classroom. The Rhode Island Federation of Teachers agrees that our students should never be subjected to ineffective teachers. We recognize the importance of high-quality evaluation in providing feedback to teachers to strengthen their instructional practice.

In the past decade, after securing more than $3 million dollars in grants from the American Federation of Teachers, the Rhode Island Foundation, the US Department of Education and the Gates Foundation, the RIFTHP has convened a consortium of our locals, in collaboration with their local school administrators, to develop and implement a comprehensive teacher evaluation system. This ongoing process has provided hundreds of hours of training to thousands of teachers and hundreds of school administrators at no cost to the districts. In addition to providing valuable feedback to support the improvement of classroom instruction, the evaluation provides districts valuable objective data to make personnel decisions.

In addition, under the direction of our director of professional issues we offer continuous professional development opportunities for our members. We strongly believe that supporting our teachers' professional growth throughout their career is an important role of our union and helps to create and sustain a stronger professional workforce. Like Mr. Marra, the RIFTHP strives to support a high-performing and well-equipped teaching force. Our children deserve nothing less.

While Mr. Flynn held steadfast to a brief history lesson in the evolution of collective bargaining laws passed in Rhode Island, it would seem obvious that he is defending the status quo. Excellence is not born of following the status quo. Leadership is not born of following the status quo. Our children's education is more important than following the status quo.

Confession Number Five

Over the years I have had a number of students with various physical disabilities. Many years ago, I had a sharp, kind student, who had a hearing disability and needed me to wear a small microphone that helped the student hear during class. This was not the first time I had such a student. One day I excused myself for a moment under the guise that I had to check for a piece of important mail I was expecting. In truth, I had to use the bathroom. As I walked in the teacher's mailroom, which is right next to the bathroom, I was greeted by a colleague who immediately went into a rant about what a waste of time the previous afternoon's faculty meeting had been. This colleague was upset about how particular teachers wasted time with a host of needless questions and unnecessary comments. Names were thrown around at will. I listened and then excused myself to use the bathroom. Upon returning to class it suddenly dawned on me that the student wearing the hearing aids had heard the entire discussion, and God knows what in the bathroom! I quickly and quietly went over to the student and apologized, to which the student responded, "Don't worry, I hear it all the time."

Chapter Six
Teacher Pensions and Promises Broken

I learned the value of hard work by working hard.
~ Margaret Mead

In planning this book, I did not set out to address the topic of teacher re-tirement systems. Teacher pensions, after all, have little or nothing to do with what happens in the classroom. My thinking changed as I pondered how the public pension crisis has impacted millions of teachers, and how the existence of this crisis sheds light on the intersection of public schools and politics.

This crisis threatens many towns, cities and states across the country, straining budgets and depriving teachers of income they were counting on in retirement. Retirees have been forced to rearrange their finances at a stage in life where few if any options exist.

Teachers and taxpayers appear to be the biggest losers in this high-stakes drama, created mainly by a tandem of politicians and labor unions that de-manded more generous pay for their members while promising votes for pol-iticians who cooperated. With such ingredients, it's not hard to understand how this debacle became a national story.

A brief history on Rhode Island's pension crisis—how it evolved, and what has been done about it—may provide some insight into what has happened, or is happening, in other states.

Rhode Island's pension system, created in 1936, "sprang out of the noblest of intentions: to compensate retired workers for long years of comparatively low-wage government work." Over time, the system merged Rhode Island state workers with public school teachers and became known as the Employees' Retirement System of Rhode Island, or ERSRI.

The problems started slowly and built up over time. I recall in the early 1990s, not long after I started teaching, Rhode Island lawmakers passed retirement and pension legislation that had disastrous long-term implications. But by then, the state was already headed for a fiscal disaster.

Decades before I started teaching, state lawmakers had started passing "special retirement bills" or "one-person retirement deals" that favored certain people—evidently those who knew someone who could get legislation passed to boost their individual pensions. These "special bills" or "giveaways," as many have referred to them, started in earnest during the 1960s and 70s and then exploded during the 1980s and early 90s. At the same time, passive if not derelict overview by elected officials, and unrealistic assumptions about the fund's growth prospects, contributed to what became, by 2010, a financial time bomb.

Katherine Gregg, a well-respected *Providence Journal* reporter, chronicled these missteps and preventable disasters in 1991, in a famous series of articles titled "Set for Life," which called the 1980s a "decade-long binge of generosity." One of those articles, "SPECIAL DEALS: How the State Took Care of Its Own" (March 31, 1991), described how over the previous ten years, state lawmakers "in more than 400 instances" had "ignored arguments about fairness' and 'sound pension funding'" as they passed "one-of-a-kind rules for favored individuals and groups."

More recently, Ted Nesi, a reporter for local station WPRI-TV, described Rhode Island's pension fiasco as "a maddening chronicle of a crisis foretold." In a December 19, 2012 article, "How Lawmakers, Union Leaders Jeopardized the RI Pension Fund," Nesi described how "annual benefits paid out more than tripled" during the 1980s, "from $42 million in 1980 to $136 million in 1990—rising far more quickly than inflation or the rest of the state budget." This was just the beginning of how "a shortfall pegged at roughly $2.3 billion in 1986 nearly tripled to $6.8 billion" before Rhode Island's pension overhaul in 2011.

Part of this binge, Nesi wrote, allowed "retired state workers and teachers to begin receiving cost-of-living adjustments (COLAs) in 1981 which increased pensions by 3 percent each year." Lawmakers also softened age and service requirements. As a result, by the end of the decade, a pension that had been available only at age fifty-five after thirty years of service was now available at any age after twenty-eight years of service.

Nesi notes that "some union officials voiced doubts, but they ceased when legislative leaders dropped the work requirement for a pension from thirty years, down to twenty-eight years." In other words, they willingly bought into a plan that deposited less money into the pension fund even as it increased the amount the plan would have to pay out. Yes, you read that sentence correctly. A major pension problem was all but guaranteed. With dire consequences, many members of Rhode Island's General Assembly continued to kick the can down the road.

An older gentleman (wishing to remain anonymous) who was a young lobbyist when much of this costly legislation was passed remembers being in the office of a leading politician of the day and listening as someone pointed out that the math involved in such generous benefits did not add up. It was clear to this conscientious objector that the pension fund would not be able to honor its commitments to future retirees. The leading politician simply remarked, "That's for future legislators to figure out. I've got my votes and re-election donations from passing this legislation and that's all I care about." This self-serving response provides more than a little insight into the origins of a system that was all but guaranteed to fail.

Yet Nesi writes: "Officials said they weren't worried about the combination of fewer assets and rising costs, even though the fund was already paying out more annually than it was taking in." And other politicians "weren't worried because they simply didn't know what was going on."

This is a copout, of course. Politicians claiming to not know what is going on in their own chambers is akin to employees not knowing what their job requires of them. Among those who were apparently unaware was then-Council 94 President Thomas Chellel, who was also a member of the Retirement Board. When asked by a *Providence Journal* reporter if he knew that the pension fund had a negative cash flow, Chellel said no, but he added that now that someone had brought it to his attention, he was "concerned."

The political culture in Rhode Island has a history of entitlement and cronyism, and that is reflected in what happened with the state's pension system. Gregg wrote that during the 1980s "roughly 1,190 retirement bills" were "introduced...to make special rules for individuals. At least 406 of these bills passed in one form or another. Hundreds of other individuals benefitted from 'generic' bills, with no names attached."

A few examples from Gregg's "Set for Life" series shed further light on the scope and scale of Rhode Island's self-serving political culture during the 1980s:

> "J. Troy Earhart, Commissioner of Elementary and Secondary Education, was allowed to buy credit for two decades of out-of-state work for which he already received $18,087 a year in pension benefits from Massachusetts." With those credits, Earhart was expected to leave state employment "with another pension of at least $58,176 a year," bringing his combined pensions to a "potential $76,263."

> "James Rigney, who had already worked four decades for Brown & Sharpe when he came out of retirement to serve as (Governor Edward) DiPrete's Director of Labor...left the Director's job four years later, with an annual pension of at least $19,142, the amount someone else at the same salary level might get after seventeen years on the job."

> "Former Rep. William Hobson, D-Cumberland, was able to make a one-time payment of about $67.50 that boosted his pension benefits by an estimated $3,185 a year."

> "Former University of Rhode Island Prof. Aaron J. Alton was allowed to buy credit for six of the years he taught at Miami University in Ohio at a special rate pegged to his entry-level salary. Alton was billed $2,020, far short of the $72,521 he would have paid if he had been charged the 'full actuarial cost.'"

When Gregg asked former state Sen. William Irons about such deals, Irons responded: "Everybody was getting money back then. The state was awash in spending that we probably regret now. There was an attitude that we could afford anything, so a lot of programs that might not have been approved otherwise made it through because people weren't as concerned about how much it cost."

Nesi adds to the story, describing how the state Retirement Board voted in 1989 to lower the investment return forecast to 7.5 percent—a wise move, given the strains on the system and the uncertainty that always surrounds a pension fund's investment returns. But the change was short-lived. Just a year later, in the spring of 1990, then-House Speaker Joseph DeAngelis stepped in and strongly suggested the board should revisit the decision. Under pressure, the board voted on June 13 to raise the return forecast to 8 percent. That was not the end of it. In 1998, the board raised the forecast again, this time to 8.25 percent, where it remained until 2011.

Nesi tells us that "DeAngelis had a good reason for caring about an arcane actuarial formula – budget talks between DiPrete and legislative Democrats had deadlocked, and raising the return meant the General Assembly could cut its yearly contribution to the pension system fund by as much as $12 million." According to Katherine Gregg's reporting, DeAngelis said he got the idea for the instant savings from the state's auditor general, Anthony Piccirilli.

Politicians might use such accounting irregularities so they can claim to have lowered government costs while in office, and thus gain greater public trust. But elevating the projected rate of return on the pension fund forces investments in higher risk assets which, generally speaking, means stocks. Accordingly, if the stock market stalls or retreats, this dangerous actuarial formula will hurt the fund rather than help it.

Nesi writes that 1990 was "the second year in a row lawmakers balanced the budget by putting less money into the pension fund." They would do so again in 1991, and again during a state banking crisis that followed soon thereafter. As a result, tens of millions of dollars in contributions never made it into the pension fund and therefore did not accumulate interest that would have helped to pay for future retiree benefits.

Some have gone so far as to describe the lobbying for, and passage of, such unrealistic policies as criminal. But not every elected official in state government went along with these short-sighted, self-serving pieces of legislation. Over the years, a few brave officials, along with a variety of business leaders and other interested parties, raised concerns about the health and well-being of the pension fund.

As Gregg reported, the state Retirement Board issued a "once-a-year objection to 'all private special interest retirement bills," arguing that "these bills are against all sound pension principles." Among the objectors was Nancy Mayer, who was elected General Treasurer of Rhode Island in 1994 and re-elected in 1996. I interviewed Mayer twice in August of 2018. Her recollections of shady deal making and insight into Rhode Island's political culture were both enlightening and disturbing.

She marveled at how "unbelievably bad" the state's political climate was, but of her own time in office, she says she had "no ulterior motives other than to do what she thought was best for the people of Rhode Island." Re-election was never a concern.

Her altruism was severely tested, however. On one occasion, she refused to back a plan to sell bonds that were supposed to fund a portion of the pension system's unfunded liability. When she asked how issuing pension obligation bonds would impact the pension system, a high-ranking senator responded with a flurry of negative comments and even threatened Mayer that she was "going to jail" if she didn't sign. She quickly told the senator to, by all means, "get the police."

Mayer was concerned that the rate of return from the bond proceeds would not offset the risk and the cost of capital to the pension fund. Such a scenario, called "negative arbitrage," occurs when the amount one has borrowed and now owes will exceed what the money borrowed will gain on its investment. For example, if the interest to be paid on the bonds was 5 percent and the interest gained from the investment was 3 percent, there is a net negative of 2 percent.

Mayer also understood that the brokers chosen to execute these bond sales would make healthy commissions. She was concerned about who would choose the brokers and how that process might play out politically and financially.

"It's kind of fun to be a happy warrior," she said. "I had a fiduciary responsibility to the pensioners and the people of Rhode Island to act in their best interest and I believe I did my job."

Licensed actuaries shared these concerns and also raised others. Unfortunately, voices of pragmatism and reason were often drowned out by legislators and union officials, who were given high marks for securing unrealistically generous benefits for their constituents. Of course, securing high marks as a legislator and union official usually translates into re-election and job security, respectively. But not telling the truth about the negative, mathematical realities involved with dozens of highly questionable pension-related bills and issues is the moral equivalent of lying by omission. All of these bills had future consequences and commitments attached to them.

As noted, the history of Rhode Island's pension fund probably sounds familiar to many people across the country. One telling indicator, from the credit rating agency Moody's, suggested that as of January 2018, "local, state and federal governments are about $7 trillion short in funding coming pension payments." There are no quick or easy solutions to such massive short falls.

The Great Recession of 2007 to 2009 contributed to this shortfall, resulting in a 55 percent drop in the stock market, which simply ravaged equity investments. By 2010, Rhode Island's pension fund was beyond any hope of carrying through on promises made to current pensioners, as well as future retirees.

It was against this dismal backdrop, in 2011, that then-Rhode Island General Treasurer (and now Governor) Gina Raimondo released a report titled "TRUTH IN NUMBERS: The Security and Sustainability of Rhode Island's Retirement System." Raimondo's report outlined the forces that had driven the Rhode Island pension system to the brink of disaster. More important, it spelled out the painful steps needed to resurrect the fund so current and future retirees could once again have faith that their retirements were on sure footing. Wisely, Raimondo approached this as a math problem and did not point fingers or name names regarding who did what in the past. She kept the conversations professional and stuck to what needed to be done.

Of course, part of the daunting challenge was in telling these same public servants that their benefits, though they will be more secure, will not be what they were once promised. This is especially difficult when the person conveying the message is an elected official. Many people blame the messenger, but blaming Raimondo for sounding a loud alarm and having the wherewithal to host meetings in nearly all of Rhode Island's 39 cities and towns to explain the dire situation and the unpopular solutions is misguided, even if it stems from genuine frustration.

One of the important lessons history teaches us is that we must often wait a generation or two to assess the impact of significant legislation. That no meaningful reform had occurred before Raimondo initiated change is telling of Rhode Island's political culture, and it is understandable that some pensioners and future pensioners were angry about the changes. But those who blame Raimondo for diminished pensions would do well to contemplate how such a horrible situation developed over the preceding thirty years.

In her report, Raimondo recognized that any proposed reform would have "immediate and direct consequences for hardworking state employees and teachers, who have done nothing wrong and contributed what was asked of them to the pension system."

"The problem does not lie with them," she said, but with "a poorly designed system that has been faltering for decades."

Raimondo also recognized that another group of people had to be considered: "the hardworking Rhodes Islanders outside the pension system, who are struggling to save for their own retirements, and are being asked to pay higher taxes, in good part, to fund the pension system."

Finally, she noted that all Rhode Islanders would suffer "if the state has to make severe cuts to vital public services to maintain the current pension system."

One phrase often used in the discussion of pensions is "unfunded liability." In brief, this refers to the difference between a plan's obligations and its assets. Naturally, as the unfunded liability grows, it becomes more difficult for the fund to fulfill its promises to recipients.

Raimondo's "TRUTH IN NUMBERS" report outlines five key drivers of Rhode Island's structural pension deficit:

1. The state failed to use "sound actuarial practices." Rather than follow the advice of actuarial experts, the state made "key decisions" that "had the effect of lowering contributions into the retirement system." As the report notes, "as early as 1974, the actuary for the pension system warned the General Assembly that it was not paying proper attention to the economic health of the pension plan:

Continuously mounting actuarial deficits, if not viewed with complacency, are at least not considered with the degree of concern which such a situation demands...Perhaps, mingled with these attitudes is the feeling that though future generations of employees may be affected, the problem is of no concern to present employees, a sort of let the future take care of itself' psychology. Whatever may be the reason behind this lack of official and employee concern, the fact is that it is unrealistic. A change of attitude and remedial and corrective measures are imperative if the retirement system is to survive and fulfill its functions and stated objective for present employees as well as future participants.

One would think that an objective and fiscally responsible report like this would have gained the attention of the elected officials who were in a position to act. Rhode Island had no such luck. As noted above, against advice from actuaries to lower the fund's projected rate of return to no higher than 8 percent, officials raised it to 8.25. This placed added pressure on the Retirement Board to produce higher gains, forcing it to take on riskier investments. It would have been far safer to use 5 to 7 percent as an assumed rate of return. Having extra money is preferable to having less money when you promised more. But as the report stated, "unrealistically optimistic assumptions increased the unfunded liability."

2. From the 1960s through the 1980s, the state approved "generous benefit improvements without corresponding taxpayer or employee contributions." At the same time, the state reduced normal retirement eligibility "from age 60 and/or 38 years of service, to 28 years of service with no age requirement."

These changes bring to light an important concept in pension accounting known as "normal cost," which is "the amount required to be paid in any given year to fund the cost of pension benefits earned during the year." Normal cost must work with an assumed rate of return on the fund's investment in order to have the appropriate amount of money to pay retiree benefits. Unfortunately for employees, the assumed rate of return was too aggressive at 8.25 percent, and the deposits into the fund fell short of the normal cost. This double negative went on for decades, with dire consequences for retirees and taxpayers alike.

3. Rhode Island's pension system allowed retired public employees to "routinely earn retirement benefits that exceed 100 percent of their final average earnings" after just several years of retirement.

Pension checks in the range of 60-80 percent of an employee's average pay during the final three to five years of work were common. And cost-of-living adjustments (COLA's) granted at 3 percent, compounded annually, often elevated retirees' pensions to more than 100 percent of their final earnings, adding to the stress on the pension fund.

As the report put it: "the true normal cost for nearly all employees and retirees" was never "fully contributed to the system."

4. With retirees living longer, many were outliving old mortality rates, placing greater stress on the pension fund.

5. Investment returns failed to meet overly optimistic goals. From 2001 to 2010 the Rhode Island pension fund earned an average annual rate of return of 2.28 percent, while the assumed rate of return was 8.25 percent. The Great Recession and subsequent stock market plunge certainly did not help matters, nor did the stock market decline in 2001-2002. As noted above, using more conservative assumed rates of return in the range of 5 to 7 percent would have protected against the potential for disappointment in a down market.

For perspective, consider that the average annual return on the Standard & Poor's 500 index was "just under 6.5 percent" (assuming all dividends were reinvested) from 2001 to 2018. By using lower investment return projections such as 5 to 7 percent, we can be more confident that our goals will be achieved, while any shortfalls are diminished.

The 2011 pension overhaul impacted retirees who had counted on specific monthly incomes and COLAs for the rest of their lives. Additionally, soon-to-retire workers were forced to work more years and accept smaller monthly pensions than they had been promised for two decades or more. What else could the Rhode Island General Assembly do after Raimondo released her report, along with actuarially sound proposals, than to address the pension fund's glaring deficiencies? Doing nothing was not an option, unless one wished to see the fund fall into insolvency. All other options involved reduced benefits. Raimondo, in an effort to save the pension fund, chose difficult yet financially sound principles over a collapse of the entire system. She sacrificed heavy political capital while engineering a more realistic and healthy fund for retirees and future retirees.

This kind of bold altruism reminds me of a wonderful quote by the ancient Roman Emperor, Marcus Aurelius, referring to one of his role models as a young man: "he was a man who looked to what ought to be done, and not to the reputation which is got by a man's acts." How different the world would be if everyone lived and acted in such an honorable manner.

Confession Number Six

I like to run a spirited classroom full of thoughts and questions that hopefully stimulate further discussion. Every once in a while, the conversation may "elevate" to a level where it gets a bit loud. Things might go a little sideways. Once in a great while "loud" might become a bit contentious, with banter that presents some humor, and perhaps also some bravado or colorful and not-totally-academic dialogue. I confess that I cannot remember ever getting into this kind of pithy dialogue with a female student.

Chapter Seven
The Profound Importance of Experience

Teach for America was built on the idea that our best hope for reaching 'One Day' is to have thousands of alumni use their diverse experiences and ideas to effect change from inside and outside the education system.

~Wendy Kopp
Founder, Teach for America

Experiences shape our lives. They play a key role in who we become and how we view the world. Teachers are in a position to shape powerful classroom experiences. Many times we don't even know this is happening. But as authority figures in the lives of children we must be ever mindful of the impact our thoughts, words, and deeds may have on our students.

I was fortunate enough to do some traveling during my college years. Visiting a number of countries in Europe, North Africa and the Middle East, along with a semester in Mexico, opened my mind to the profound effects that travel and learning in a different culture can have on us. I find international travel particularly interesting because we are transported out of our comfort zone and placed in other cultures with their own unique histories and traditions. History teaches us that "a person or situation can only be understood against the background of its own time." Perhaps this is why, during my first four years of teaching, I organized and led three different international trips with my students. Educational travel companies make this fairly easy for any teacher desiring to expose their students to the benefits and wonder of international travel. Kids learn so much and will never forget these experiences.

All teachers remember their first year and usually admit that it was trying in many ways. Early on in my first year I asked my department chair, Charlie Capizano, if he would be interested in chaperoning a trip I was planning to the Soviet Union, for the spring of 1987. He immediately agreed. We ended up gathering 19 students from grades 9-12 who wished to spend their spring vacation touring St. Petersburg (then known as Leningrad) and Moscow. With the Cold War still raging, the parents and students could not have been more supportive of visiting this unique country. Highlights included visiting the Winter Palace in St. Petersburg, home of the famous Hermitage Museum; touring the Peter and Paul Fortress; and then an overnight train to Moscow with tours of the Kremlin, Red Square, St. Basil's Cathedral, and Lenin's Mausoleum.

One obvious observation about Soviet life back then was how poor people were. It seemed the general population possessed little motivation. Communism had certainly dulled the spirit of the Russians we observed. Living in a meritless system had created a passive, apathetic attitude that contrasted dramatically with US market forces driven by incentives inherent in capitalism. Our students' appreciation for democracy and free market economics could not help but blossom as our trip unfolded.

It was a thrilling trip. Little did I realize then that twenty years later, I would be fortunate enough to meet Mikhail Gorbachev in person. The location: Portsmouth, Rhode Island, which is where I teach.

Mr. Gorbachev was giving a speech at a private club in town and the owner offered our school a free table for ten for the event. We quickly accepted this kind offer. Fellow teacher and friend, Jim Betres, myself, and eight students enjoyed a couple of moments with Mr. Gorbachev, who brought so much needed change and bold leadership to his ailing country.

Upon meeting Mr. Gorbachev, I handed him a Powerball lottery ticket. I told him (through his interpreter) that the drawing for this national lottery was later that evening and that I truly hoped he would win. The winning ticket would be worth some $250 million. He looked at me a bit puzzled until the interpreter finished. His grin and nod of acknowledgement will be forever etched in my mind.

Two years later I led a group of students with another fellow teacher, Emily Marrotti, to Spain and Morocco. The stark differences between the southern Spanish towns of Cordoba, Granada and Toledo and the ancient cities of Fez and Tangiers in Morocco gave students an uncommon look at two very different cultures separated by only a few miles of water, the Strait of Gibraltar. Christian Europe and Muslim North Africa presented us with the ability to compare two distinctly different cultures and continents without traveling far from either one.

The third and final international trip I led with students took place during my fourth year of teaching. I had always wanted to teach abroad and was selected to teach US and European history at an international school in Salzburg, Austria. This was the easiest trip by far. With only six students in my Advanced Placement US History class and the German town of Berchtesgaden only twenty miles away, we planned to visit the famed "Eagle's Nest," which was a 50th birthday gift to Adolf Hitler during his brutal reign. Nothing more was required beyond each student bringing their passport to class, departing in one of the school's vans to the West German border and touring the building, which now operates as a historical site. This was Hitler's mountain retreat in the Bavarian Alps, and the stunning views alone were worth the trip.

The remaining field trips have been more local in nature, but I believe each one has given students a unique and special insight.

Sometime in the mid-1990s, while teaching a unit on personal finance and investing in my economics class, I was approached by an older gentleman who substituted at our school on a regular basis. What a blessing it was to meet this generous and kind man. His name was Ed Fitzgerald and he was a retired Marine colonel who had spent many years in business after retiring from the service. Then in his late 60s, Ed had found substituting to be a meaningful way of spending many of his days in retirement. Aware that we had been studying the stock market and investing, he asked me if I'd like to bring the economics students on a field trip to the New York Stock Exchange. He had a variety of friends working security at the exchange and thought they could arrange a tour with guest speakers. I could not imagine a better field trip for economic students.

For the next fifteen years or so, Ed would touch base with his friends at both the NYSE and the Federal Reserve Bank of New York (a short five minute walk from the Exchange) and I would organize a bus rental, purchase Broadway theater tickets, secure hotel rooms and handle permission slips for some 48 students and four teacher chaperones for our annual Stock Market field trip. The trip began with an early departure on a spring Sunday morning. We would proceed directly to Chinatown and Little Italy, where the students could walk around in groups of three or more and grab lunch, purchase what they wished or just take in the sights. By 4:00 P.M. we would check into the Roosevelt Hotel, freshen up a bit and then head six blocks up to Broadway, where we would get a quick, informal dinner. Next, we would all meet thirty minutes before showtime at our designated theater. Blue Man Group was one of the favorites in the late '90s and early 2000s. We attended a number of other great Broadway shows, but Blue Man was the overall favorite.

After the show the kids were free to roam around Times Square until our 11:00 P.M. meeting time, and then we would all walk back together to our hotel. Allowing this many high school students to roam in Times Square was by far the most stressful part of the trip. Never once did we have an issue...that I ever heard about!

Monday morning, we enjoyed a gourmet breakfast buffet before departing for the 9:30 opening bell at the New York Stock Exchange. While we had studied personal finance and investing prior to our trip, entering the trading area of the exchange was an exciting experience for my students. We occupied a long, narrow platform high above the trading floor that gave spectators a particularly enhanced view of the action below. Upon the opening bell and start of trading, we would watch the action for twenty minutes or so before being led up to one of the conference rooms within the exchange, where a trader from the floor would greet us and discuss the workings of what we had just observed.

These were seasoned veterans who always left us with a few solemn words of advice and wisdom. The chaperones were just as impressed as the students as these traders took time out of their hectic morning to explain what they do. And each year, after these hour-long discussions were over, the traders confided to me that they absolutely loved talking with the kids. In fact, they felt it was important for students to understand not only the mechanics of the stock exchange, but, more importantly, the ethics and discipline behind the traders' work. Each trader spoke about taking the long view when investing in stocks and being extremely careful to not fall prey to the greed that regularly consumes people in the world of high finance and investments. This was sound advice that the students could dwell on for years to come.

By 11 A.M. we were making our way just 3 blocks north of the Exchange to the Federal Reserve Bank of New York. There, Ed's friends, who ran security for the bank, organized a tour and video about the purpose and functions of the bank. The highlight of this tour came when we descended six stories below street level to the vaults holding thousands of 22-pound blocks of gold. Countries around the world trust this vault and the security it provides with a portion of their national gold reserves.

Each student was able to hold one of the small, dense 22-pound blocks that by this printing would be roughly valued at $651,000.

By this point in my career, field trips had become a staple in planning for each year. But the best trip ever was just coming into view.

In the spring of 2006, I assigned the Pulitzer Prize winning book *John Adams* for summer reading to my AP US history students. Quite a few people whose opinions I value had strongly suggested reading this book. Written by the gifted writer/historian David McCullough, it was his second Pulitzer Prize winning book (his first was *Truman*). Little did I know what an impact this book would have on both me and my students.

My students are tested on their summer reading assignment on our first day of class. In this instance, we followed the short, twenty question test with a discussion of what the students thought of *John Adams* and the author. This book was one of the best I had ever read. Most students, for their part, marveled at the depth and breadth of the subject matter. They wondered how any writer could amass the details and vivid stories that Mr. McCullough had included. The fact that high school juniors were so impressed with a 700-page book caused me to pause and reflect. How might we further use this exceptional book as we explored Colonial American history?

On the second day of school I decided to track down Mr. McCullough and see if it might be possible to have my students meet him in person. I noticed that he had just spoken at a college in neighboring Massachusetts, so I called the school and spoke to a person familiar with its event planning. She told me that the visit was arranged through Mr. McCullough's daughter, who lived in Maine. She gave me the daughter's contact information and I called her. I explained that her father's book had impressed us all and that I was interested in trying to secure an audience with him so that my students could meet her celebrated father. I impressed upon her that we would request only an hour or so of his time and that this meeting was not intended to inconvenience him in any way. She liked the idea so much that she ended up saying, "Oh, why don't I just give you his address so you can write directly to him yourself." I readily agreed and was surprised to learn that Mr. McCullough lived nearby, on the island of Martha's Vineyard.

I quickly sat down to write a short note and mailed it after school. Much to my surprise, Mr. McCullough's secretary called me two days later, indicating that he liked the idea and would welcome the chance to speak with high school students. Needless to say, we accepted. After more phone calls to work out a date that fit our schedules we were set for a visit to Martha's Vineyard. We were to meet across the street from his home in bucolic Tisbury, at an old meeting house well preserved by the local community.

It was a gorgeous, crisp September day as some forty students, my dear friend and colleague, Mary Kate O'Keefe, and I sailed across Martha's Vineyard Sound and then boarded a bus that took us to Tisbury. Mr. McCullough met us in front of his home and walked us to the meeting house, where seating was arranged for us to have an informal talk with this wonderful gentleman and author. David McCullough is the kind of man that everyone should have for a grandfather. His sincere kindness and keen intellect, coupled with his extraordinary voice—which so many of us have listened to in documentaries such as Ken Burns' *Civil War*—helped to remind us that we were in the presence of an authentic American icon.

Mr. McCullough's love of history and willingness to humbly share his knowledge quickly grabbed the students' attention. He opened the discussion with a brief history of the old building we were seated in, taking the time to talk about the people who made the building possible so many years ago. Massive trees had to be felled, whereafter mill workers sawed the great logs, carpenters worked by hand, and countless hours were taken to erect this handsome old building.

After an hour or so of dialogue and questions, Mr. and Mrs. McCullough invited us to their home across the street for a drink and a showing of their gorgeous backyard that abuts a nature preserve. His current office is housed in a newer, shingled structure separate from the house, adorned with a desk, two couches and shelves filled with an array of books. It was a beautiful space to work in.

Later, he invited us all to follow him to the very back of his yard, to a rather small, ordinary looking shed-like structure. This is where Mr. McCullough came when he wanted peace and no interruptions. There on a small desk sat his old-style typewriter. He said he preferred using an old typewriter rather than word processing because he could actually see the hard copy as it evolved and didn't have to worry about losing it, and I quote, "to wherever it went once one presses save." Who can argue with a gentleman in possession of two Pulitzer Prizes? The students loved his honesty and old-school devotion.

While showing us this small office he remarked that, at times, he would sit at his desk, hands folded behind his neck, his face looking up at the ceiling. Occasionally, he would notice a family member had strolled out to see if he needed anything and, upon seeing him deep in thought, they would retreat quietly so as not to disturb him while he was contemplating. He then looked at the students and told them with a wink, "at those moments when I was supposedly in deep thought, I didn't have a single, solitary thought in my head!" His honesty was precious.

Our visit ended with a bouncing ferry ride back across Martha's Vineyard Sound to Falmouth, where our bus awaited us. Every student knew that this meeting with one of the great American writers of our time was a unique, once-in-a-lifetime experience. I must add that our venture that day could not have happened without the help of Mr. McCullough's secretary, Gail Moan, and his kind wife, Rosalie, as well as that of the gifted literary giant himself.

I often try to remind my students about creating opportunities and reference a famous quote by the great hockey player, Wayne Gretsky, who said: "You miss one hundred percent of the shots you don't take." No doubt, good fortune and luck played their roles, but this audience with Mr. McCullough evolved from simply taking a shot.

One more field trip to visit a celebrated local author, Nathaniel Philbrick, followed shortly after the trip to David McCullough's home. Mr. Philbrick, now a nationally acclaimed author, lives on nearby Nantucket Island. We read his wildly adventurous book, *In the Heart of the Sea*, which recounts the gruesome trip of Nantucket whalers who were rammed and sunk by a massive sperm whale in the Pacific Ocean in 1819. This true story gave rise to Herman Melville's *Moby Dick* a few decades later.

Mr. Philbrick was kind enough to arrange a meeting for us at a local church and spoke to us about the depth and breadth of work involved in researching and writing such an interesting historical account. That we ventured to the very island where the sailors departed from and meandered through the streets of their quaint, cobble-stoned town certainly enhanced the experience for many. He reminded us of the importance of recasting the context of the times in which these sailors lived back in the early 1800s. These were simple, local men venturing halfway around the world on an 85-foot boat because they were trying to make a living for their families. Mr. Philbrick asked the students what they thought it must have been like for twenty-one men living two-to-four years together on that small boat. He painted vivid pictures in the students' minds about undernourished, dehydrated men facing what appeared to be endless days, weeks and months, crammed together on a ship less than 100 feet long.

While everyone in our group had read this book, Mr. Philbrick took the time to explain the countless hours of research needed before one ever begins to organize the actual writing of such a story. Hundreds of hours of independent research and thinking was something most students had never considered.

Watching students as they listen to people like Mikhail Gorbachev, David McCullough and Nathaniel Philbrick is a precious thing for any teacher to observe. But all teachers have countless wonderful community members at their fingertips who would love to give a presentation to local students. Most of the time all this takes is some thought and a kind request. I urge teachers to take a shot. You'll never know unless you do.

The latest "annual" field trip that has emerged over the past five years is a long but fruitful day trip, via plane, to Gettysburg National Park in Pennsylvania. This trip is the culmination of our reading of the Pulitzer Prize-winning novel by Michael Shaara, *Killer Angels*. It is based on the three-day battle at Gettysburg, PA in 1863. This battle is viewed by many historians as a key turning point in the Civil War and a crippling blow to the Confederate South.

The idea for this trip came from my wife, Maria. We were touring colleges in the Washington, DC, and Pennsylvania area with our daughter, Kate. Gettysburg College was on the list and it was an easy drive from Baltimore-Washington International Airport, which has reasonable roundtrip airfares from Providence. Maria knew we had read *Killer Angels* and thought this would be a fun, unique way to wrap up our study of the Civil War. She was right.

Each year, a day in early November is selected and some thirty to forty students, along with a couple of my colleagues as chaperones, take an early flight to Baltimore. Upon landing we board a waiting tour bus, and proceed to Gettysburg National Park for a wonderful private tour of the entire battlefield. With our professional guide, students are able to better visualize the scale and perspective faced by the two warring armies on those first three days of July back in 1863. Actual bullet holes and cannon balls are still embedded in a few buildings. Replica fences are set in the fields that make up this distinctly hallowed ground born from our darkest hours. This trip really does have the effect of making history come alive for the students. The tour guides do a superb job of bringing the past to life with vivid descriptions and detailed explanations. And they especially enjoy it when they get a group that has read extensively on the battle before visiting.

An amusing thing happened during our first trip to Gettysburg. Upon boarding the plane for our return flight to Providence, the captain asked if the class president, Kathryn Stack, would join him at the front of the plane. He asked her if she would be comfortable speaking to the entire plane, to which a surprised Kathryn agreed and was given a script, line by line. As Kathryn recounted years later, "After I finished the announcement (which included weather in Providence, flight duration and expected conditions] I was allowed to sit in the cockpit. The pilot told me to bring up a friend and so Katie (Barry) came with me. He took our picture sitting in the pilot seats!" She also remembers "laughing through the announcements as I could hear my classmates laughing, but could not see them."

One of the byproducts of organizing field trips is unplanned encounters like this one. The more things we involve ourselves in, the more opportunities there are for unique and unplanned scenes like this to play out.

Planning for this trip gets a bit tricky with airfares constantly changing. Choosing a particular day when all permission slips are due, along with a non-refundable check, usually allows us to lock in a firm price on airfare by that afternoon. All other components—bus transportation to and from Gettysburg, lunch, and guided tour—are on a per-person basis. So far, we've been fortunate to keep the price below $300 per student with everything included. Equally fortunate, I have always been able to find donations so that no student ever missed out because of the cost.

Confession Number Seven

Kindness matters. When I think of the highest quality teachers I have ever had or taught with, it seems they have all been, first and foremost, kindhearted and good people. Their knowledge of subject matter and ability to teach effectively were a given. But it was their kindness, when combined with their unquestioned command of their discipline, that made them the teacher of choice for so many students.

Chapter Eight
Bright Developments on the Horizon

"There are two ways of spreading light: to be the candle or the mirror that reflects it."

~ Edith Wharton

As I write this book, there are signs of hope.

Tenure, seniority, and due process—in their historic forms—are being challenged around the country by progressive thinking governors, mayors and elected school board members, as well as teachers, principals and superintendents. At the very least, modifying these three tenets of teacher contracts seems more than overdue. This doesn't have to mean eliminating them.

Some other signs of hope:

- There is now a national discussion about basing teacher retention and even pay on legitimate teacher evaluations.
- A growing number of superintendents and school principals are gaining broader latitude to decide teacher placement based on teacher qualifications, rather than just seniority—a change from the decades when a teacher's certification determined where a teacher would be placed in a school.
- Due process, as written and carried out in teacher contracts, is probably the single most formidable obstacle in removing a poorly performing teacher. But a growing number of organizations and individuals are taking on the more regressive elements within the

teacher union establishment by raising concerns and asking honest questions, such as: Who benefits from this exceptional level of employment protection? And who loses?

Where due process in removing an ineffective teacher historically has taken two to three years and cost hundreds of thousands of dollars, a more reasonable and fair time frame of two to four weeks is being presented by many as more than enough time to reach a conclusion. To be clear, every teacher deserves due process. But the language and timetable in most union contracts virtually guarantees a long, drawn-out and costly battle that school boards end up deeming unaffordable.

At the heart of the matter is teacher accountability. Effective and efficient evaluations will inevitably shine light on the countless dedicated, hardworking teachers who succeed in multiple ways to enhance the daily classroom experience for their students. And that is a light worth shining and celebrating. Effective, vibrant teachers in our schools far outnumber those who make up the unfortunate minority of poor performers! Teacher accountability will be a compelling force for change that guarantees we will have our most effective teachers in the classroom. Yes, there is much to be optimistic about in public education as we enter the third decade of the 21st century.

Information compiled by the National Council on Teacher Quality, led by its vision that "every child deserves effective teachers, and every teacher deserves the opportunity to become an effective teacher," indicates that meaningful change is taking place with regard to using seniority as a factor in determining which teachers to lay off during a reduction in force. As figure 8.1 shows, just six states have retained seniority as the only factor. Four states indicate seniority must be considered. Twenty say seniority can be considered among other factors. Two do not allow seniority to be considered and the remaining eighteen states allow for each district within the state to decide for itself.

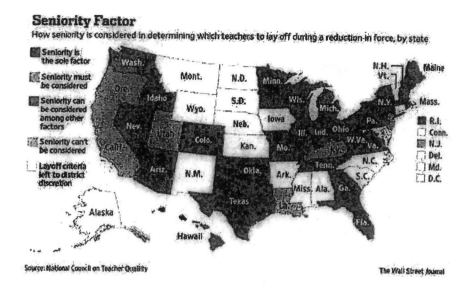

Seniority Factor

How seniority is considered in determining which teachers to lay off during a reduction-in force, by state

Source: National Council on Teacher Quality

The Wall Street Journal

The Council points to Florida, Indiana and Colorado as having so-called best practice policies, where classroom performance is a "top criterion" to be considered in layoff decisions. This is refreshing to say the least.

Tenure is changing as well. To those who work in the private sector, the very thought of not including teacher performance in deciding tenure seems negligent at best. Whether tenure will be decided after only three years of service to a community is an unanswered question. But a reasonable solution might begin with school boards and unions meeting somewhere in the middle. Since these entities won't be disappearing any time soon, this will require a collaborative effort.

As stated, tenure for teachers guarantees an incredibly powerful level of job security, something few professions come close to providing. It's too powerful. With this in mind, why not grant tenure after seven years of proven quality teaching with valid, measurable indicators? Tenure will last for up to seven years before it must be renewed, say, in year six. Why after six years? If a teacher is deemed undesirable for another seven-year run, they have a full year left in their current tenure track to seek employment elsewhere. This seems more than fair. In this model, both the community and teacher have a more level playing field on which to operate. The community is not committed to a lifetime-tenured teacher it doesn't care for, nor is a teacher entitled to professional lifetime-employment after a mere three years of acceptable service. Moreover, teachers have an incentive to constantly perform at their very highest level. In this dynamic, students, as well as teachers, will benefit.

Rethinking tenure, seniority, cumbersome layers of due process, and even merit-based pay has the potential to unleash an impressive amount of pent-up energy. Students will gain the most. Reinvigorated teachers, administrators, and school boards will benefit. As a practical matter, our nation must embrace these kinds of changes if our children are to be competitive in the global economy. Each nation's hope lies in the balance of how well we educate our youth.

The changes and reforms discussed above will not come easy. At the core of this discussion, we are talking about a culture change. Culture is everything. Good leaders know this intuitively and they create the culture they desire in whatever organization they run.

Culture change in teacher unions has been particularly slow and problematic. This is due in large part to decades of entrenched belief that the union's way is the best way. Any person or organization that challenges union policy or culture is usually deemed anti-teacher and shouted down by regressive, close-minded, staunch union supporters. Accordingly, open-minded leadership that has been sorely lacking in teacher unions holds the greatest hope for meaningful, productive change. Kinder and more thoughtful union members are beginning to make their voices heard. More books and articles challenging teacher union contract language that is harmful to student learning are finding their way to print. School boards and superintendents are demanding significant modifications to age-old policies governing hiring and firing, the lengthy and expensive layers of due process that keeps poor-performing teachers in the classroom, and performance-based teacher evaluations.

Culture change on school boards and among educational leaders hold enormous hope. Author James Kerr points out in his book *Legacy* that "a culture of asking and re-asking fundamental questions cuts away unhelpful beliefs in order to achieve clarity of execution. Humility allows us to ask a simple question: how can we do this better?" If the truth we discover from asking such uncomfortable questions brings us to an uncomfortable reality, then so be it. At the very least we have been honest with ourselves and now can make changes that will improve our schools. In the end, to become the best we can be we must, as Kerr states, be "value-based and purpose-driven."

Driving home the importance of culture change is imperative in organizations that are serious about improving. Will Hogg, operator of a Geneva-based management consultancy that helps large organizations change their cultures, uses a Japanese proverb:

"Vision without action is a dream.
Action without vision is a nightmare."

Yes, transformational thinking and leadership are needed from teachers, school boards, unions, superintendents, principals, parents and all other stakeholders. The good news is that this is happening in various stages throughout the country.

Confession Number Eight

From time to time it becomes inevitable that some type of embarrassing situation will arise in a classroom. When a student has unwittingly asked a question with double or triple meanings, or someone has envisioned a scenario where an embarrassing outcome they never contemplated is all but guaranteed, I do the following: there is a quick announcement that I have probably misunderstood what was just said, and that we will not be taking that issue on right now. Also promised is that it won't be on the next quiz or test. And then we quickly move on with the lesson at hand!

Chapter Nine
A Few More Confessions

"Education should provide the tools for a widening and deepening of life, for increased appreciation of all one sees or experiences. It should equip a person to live well, to understand what is happening about him: for to live well one must live with awareness."

~ Louis L'Amour
Author, The Education of a Wandering Man

When I began my career in teaching, I didn't think it would last more than five or six years. I had majored in history at Colby College and fulfilled the education requirements to secure my teaching certificate. My student teaching assignments during college were successful, yet I was unsure if teaching would actually be my long-term career. In the fall of 1986, I thought about my career somewhat like the former Soviet Union went about addressing its economy—in "five-year plans." I figured I'd teach for five years and then assess whether five more years seemed appropriate.

I confess that while teaching has been my chosen career, it has not been my only career. When I was growing up my family owned two nursing homes, and these businesses demanded constant, daily attention. Few businesses operate around the clock, every day of the year. And caring for our elderly, many suffering physically and emotionally, and in the twilight of their lives, presents a variety of challenges. With 256 residents to care for and nearly 300 employees to manage, running the family business was one of the last things I wished to do. But rarely do things work out as we envision.

Within a year of graduating from college, and during my first year of teaching, I found myself left in charge of running the family businesses. The sequence of events that brought this about was not good. When I entered college, my family consisted of my mother, father and two older brothers. My mother passed away during my freshman year. Four years later, during my first year of teaching, my father and oldest brother passed away. They had been running the two businesses. Prior to my father's death, I was the sibling designated as president of the companies and executor of his will upon his passing.

I was able to continue my teaching career and run the businesses thanks to the good fortune of hiring a manager who was a passionate and consummate executive in the healthcare field. Finding and retaining the services of a gifted manager made all the difference in the world.

At some point, the smaller of the two nursing homes was sold. I then bought my brother's remaining shares of the larger facility, assuming full ownership.

To say this first year of teaching was a unique and interesting one might be a gross understatement. Like so many teachers, I remember my first year with varying degrees of trepidation: steep learning curves, a victory or two, and probably a good bit of head shaking. I can't imagine a teacher who doesn't cringe in disbelief at some story from his or her first year. I remember getting so completely fed up with a young, seemingly obstinate ninth grader that I walked over to his desk, grabbed three or four of his books, launched them on to the counter next to him and said, a trifle loudly, "Can you hear me now?" Head shaking indeed. But it was also a rewarding year in that I really enjoyed having my own classroom for the first time. A clear sense of classroom ownership begins to develop in new teachers, one that goes beyond what they experienced while student teaching.

A teacher must be committed to his or her calling a solid three to five years in order to acquire a realistic picture of the profession. As my three to five years came and went, I began to see a longer stay in the profession as a real possibility. Thirty-five years later, I can't imagine having chosen a more rewarding career. Each day affords so many opportunities to elevate young minds, introduce new ways of thinking and affirm young people for their uniqueness and spirit. By the end of my first "five-year plan" it was evident to me that teaching was a welcomed calling and career.

Another confession I need to make regards my wife, Maria. She is the one who steered me to a much more student-oriented and lively teaching style than I would ever have arrived at on my own. I used to teach pretty much how

I was taught. When I was a student taking history classes, lecture and note taking was fairly standard. The teacher talks and puts notes on the board and students listen and copy the notes. While this works and brings some overall understanding of the material to students, it can also be boring and exhausting for both student and teacher.

Maria is referred to as the "quality control person" in our house, and at her suggestion, along with some discussion and key examples of how to improve the delivery of material, I altered how I taught a typical lesson. The key to Maria's pedagogy was to get the students much more involved in the actual lesson by creating a numbered, skeletal outline of questions that would take up the entire whiteboard. On a typical day there might be twelve to eighteen questions awaiting students as they enter the classroom. They understand that it is up to them to fill in the board with complete answers. Then, as we cover each of the questions during class, whoever wrote the response must read and explain their answer before the class. I may also ask a question that forces a deeper analysis. For example, I might ask, "To what extent?" or "Give another example of how this affected people of this time." In this way, our class begins in a quiet, reflective manner with students at the board filling in material from their reading and notes. It also gives me a chance to check in with kids who may have missed a class or need a few minutes of my time before we start the lesson.

Often, three or four of the numbered questions are nothing more than a reminder to me to read aloud a selected excerpt from one of many books I keep on hand to accentuate the issue or theme we may be studying. I keep perhaps 100 to 125 books on or next to my desk for just this purpose. Kids love relevant examples that make the material come alive. Well-chosen excerpts from gifted authors like David McCullough, John Meacham, Nathaniel Philbrick, Doris Kearns Goodwin, Michael Sharra, Henry David Thoreau, Marcus Aurelius, Leo Tolstoy, Randy Pauch and Alan Taylor, to name a few, add a rich flavor and texture to our understanding and thoughts. It's also important for students to see their teachers as readers and admirers of great books. A carefully chosen excerpt, read enthusiastically by a teacher, is a powerful message for young people to observe. And when students observe that the teacher truly enjoys sharing this material then the lesson may take on an added dimension of appreciation and legitimacy.

Rounding out what awaits students on the board when they arrive is an agenda of the daily lesson, including any homework assignment(s), as well as a "Quote of the Day." The quote may be a random benevolent saying, a witty quip or just a piece of advice, with the author always noted. Again, this is just another mechanism to foster thinking. Kids seem to appreciate it.

The point here is that a good degree of the classroom success I've had is based on suggestions from Maria and her thoughts on how students learn best. Setting up the board takes considerable time each morning (or afternoon prior to leaving) but it makes a world of difference with the predictability and logic that it lends to student learning. I highly recommend using this method to organize and deliver a good portion of the material in history classes. Visual learners are particularly pleased with it, and so many of us are visual learners.

Another confession pertains to a fairly recent development. As discussed earlier, I don't agree with everything in teacher union contracts. But a solid salary package and good benefits are essential to teachers, both current and future. I believe teachers are considerably underpaid given the vital role they play in the health of our nation. Merit-based pay might be the next logical step. It would reflect the true value of dedicated teachers, and it would also help attract and retain more talented people.

Beyond the challenges posed by tenure and seniority, teacher contracts also contribute to another glaring challenge: too many sick days. My contract has afforded teachers twenty sick days per year for decades! And these sick days accumulate over the years. As I write this, I have close to 480 sick days. I'm not sure what I need them for. We also have two personal days a year to be used as needed. I understand two personal days. But twenty sick days?

Under this paradigm it is not difficult to see that some teachers might abuse these benefits. I have heard teachers who use most or all of these days each year defend the practice, with rationales ranging from, "I'm entitled to them, so why wouldn't I take them," to "If I'm given 22 days then I'm certainly going to take them." It seems there is a strong need for change regarding sick days if many teachers feel entitled to use so many. The generous number only seems to act as an incentive for certain teachers to take them. Against this backdrop I know colleagues who marvel at how often and predictably a few teachers are out "sick." The confession here is that some of us have gotten to the point of betting on which day of the week certain people will be out. For instance, if we have a long weekend coming up, there might be speculation that "so-and-so" is bound to make it longer by taking a day. Another predictor runs along the lines of whether "so-and-so" has been out lately, and if not, then surely it is a given that tomorrow or the next day sickness will strike. Some of my colleagues have become masters at predicting this kind of stuff. While this kind of confession may belie a less than professional ethos, it is done entirely behind closed doors and in an eye-rolling, semi-humorous manner. Starting off a Monday morning with a colleague calling 3-1 odds on another colleague being out that particular week brings a little levity to the day. Shooting back that the odds are more like 2-1 because they didn't take the previous Friday off speaks to both the predictability and sadness of the issue.

Of course, there are legitimate reasons for missing work from time to time. That is not the kind of situation being addressed here. The habitual taker of sick days is the issue. The contract guaranteeing so many sick days is also an issue.

Another confession worth sharing is how easy it can be, at times, to misread a student. We all misread a person or situation from time to time. Every year, the first 'Thought of the Day" on my board reads: "You don't get a second chance to make a first impression." How true. And yet first impressions can be false ones. How can we possibly gain any clear understanding of who our students really are without spending a considerable amount of time with them, or, at the very least, observing them in a variety of settings? So many times we often come to only know them as a student in our particular class. This is natural, because we all have our own private lives tugging us in different directions.

Countless times throughout my career I have been surprised, both pleasantly and sadly, at learning about other interests, particular talents or perhaps family backgrounds that shed a much deeper understanding of who some of my students are outside of the classroom. Attending non-academic events like theater, community or sporting contests helps to provide a broader picture of the depth and complexity that so many of our students possess. It's always wonderful to attend an event where we see our students shine as we never imagined. And this kind of revelation has a way of reminding us of how little we really know about so many of our students and their goals, intentions, aspirations and challenges. Watching them perform and compete in a setting of their choosing also sends a strong message that a teacher is not just a classroom entity or one-dimensional person. Kids love it when teachers attend their events. Talking about their events and how they performed also allows students to see teachers in a different light. We become more authentic to them.

On the sadder side of first impressions that can lead us to misread a student, I have often come to learn of unfortunate and heart-wrenching realities that some students live with. Whenever I can't quite figure a student out who seems to be struggling with an issue or two, ranging from schoolwork, their attitude or perhaps how they relate to their peers, I usually end up talking to their guidance counselor. Guidance counselors work under various confidentiality codes, but they can enhance a teacher's understanding about a troubled student without breaking confidentiality. Some of the stories they share can be daunting. Drug use and family crisis tend to top the list of unfortunate circumstances. It may not even be the student who is using drugs, but a sibling or a parent who is addicted and creating a damaging environment at home.

In this confession about misreading or making assumptions about students, I wish to reaffirm how important it is that we, as teachers, keep an open mind and listen to our intuitions when they may speak to us. Misreading or making assumptions can be a catalyst to learn more about a child if we are cognizant and admit we may be doing this. Talking with other professionals who know this student may help to address his or her situation.

Another confession worth noting: There are times when I believe I have let a student or class down. The cause might be a poor choice of wording on a particular subject or my own bias on a topic that should have been presented more fairly. It can also grow out of the personal chemistry generated by individuals in our charge. Each class has its own distinct character. Some classes are a sheer joy to teach, with eager and kind students who get along and respect the integrity of our mission. Other classes can pose real challenges, and this is where a teacher must be vigilant in not allowing an individual or small group to command attention that distracts or undermines the lesson(s) at hand.

Poor word choice is difficult to avoid. It's going to happen because teachers confront dozens of issues each day and are simply not going to respond at a one-hundred percent level of effectiveness every time. That said, when I have spoken in a manner that makes me stop and reflect on how I could have better addressed a particular issue or situation, I make a strong effort to correct this mistake in the very next class. Students appreciate it when a teacher admits a wrong or an inaccuracy and then moves forward. Hopefully this only happens on isolated, rare occasions. Being honest enough with oneself to admit these things and address them is the big take-away I would like to stress to future teachers.

Constant awareness of our own biases is one way to keep lessons and discussions more productive and balanced. My liberal use of reading excerpts from Howard Zinn's "A People's History of the United States" perhaps offsets my center-right-leaning interpretation of some of the economic, social and political issues we study in history. I often remind students that there are rarely only two sides to a story or issue. There are far more often six or eight or twelve perspectives and angles to possibly consider. Reminding students that there are a variety of different groups within a single political party helps them better understand and deal with inconsistencies they are bound to discover. As a teacher of history, it is all the more important to present different viewpoints and perspectives, so that students can better assess and critically analyze future materials they may come across.

Teachers can also let down a class by failing to deal with one or more students who seem destined to derail the lesson. Putting up with this kind of disruption hurts the whole class. While we cannot prevent every disruption, we can act swiftly when they occur. New teachers will learn this, and hopefully sooner than later. Removing the disruptor(s) is essential. I remember that early in my career I spent way too much time appeasing disruptive students. For the past 25 years or so I have simply given them one very clear warning and then removed them from class. When we don't do this, we cheat the majority of students who expect a sound learning experience. As an added bonus, every student is now put on notice about where the line is that should not be crossed.

Confession Number Nine

While I have written hundreds of college recommendations, I feel especially privileged when the student I am recommending will be a first-generation college graduate. I call these students "barrier breakers" and make a strong effort to sit and talk with them about the importance of the choice they are making. Encouragement goes a long way, particularly when a student is choosing a path no one in his or her family has previously chosen. One child venturing out beyond a family's traditional footpath can create amazing change, not only for the student, but for their future children. What an honor it is for a teacher to take an active role at this critical time in a student's life.

Chapter 10
Final Lessons

"Quiet the mind and the soul will speak."
~ Ma Jaya Sati Bhagavati

In thinking about what has become most vital to improving education in our schools, I have tried to reduce the countless variables down to a few worthy imperatives. Individually, each concept or principle provides a logical step toward making our schools function more efficiently and effectively. Collectively, they form a solid foundation from which any school system can provide what is truly best for the students in its care.

The principle I find most important, and one that should drive all others, originates with a fourteenth century English Franciscan friar named William of Ockham. This principle came to be Latinized and named Ockham's razor. It states that the best explanation in most matters is the simplest. In philosophical terms, a razor is a principle or rule that is given to eliminating ("shaving off") what seems least likely to be the cause of an action or actions. In other words, simpler explanations are more likely to be correct.

Ockham's razor helps us divine what is most critical to improving our education system. For me, the simplest explanation is to hire and retain the best teachers at all times. Talking about dozens of other variables that need fixing is shear folly when compared with the impact of well-trained, compassionate, knowledgeable and self-motivated teachers. A school system that sets the bar high and does not relax its expectations of teachers is in the best position to reap generous rewards for its students. This also means removing lackluster and poor-performing teachers.

My second imperative: Be bold! Joseph Futoma, one of the most gifted students I've ever had, told me this when he learned I was thinking about writing a book on education. Joe graduated from Dartmouth College in three years and is currently getting his PhD in mathematics at Duke University. Being bold is the second key element that will drive change. School committees must be bold in demanding the elimination of teacher contract language that makes it so incredibly difficult and expensive to remove poor performing teachers. Forcing this issue out into the open during contract talks will shed positive light on school committees. It will also expose glaring contradictions between what teacher unions claim to seek and support and what they do, in fact, support. Their contractual guarantees work to the extreme detriment of our students, as well as parents, taxpayers and committed teachers. No well-regarded teacher supports retaining those who undermine the teaching profession. All teachers suffer when poor-performing teachers remain a fixture in our schools.

This is why it is important for school boards, superintendents and other stakeholders to be bold enough to demand and secure what is best for our children. Bold means addressing issues like tenure, seniority and countless layers of "due process," even though that may cause a backlash and angst from people and organizations used to dictating their own terms. Keeping in mind what is in our students' best interests will easily offset any unpleasantness experienced in the doing.

For example, a school board might use the refusal by the union to address these issues in contract negotiations as a "nonstarter." This means negotiations go nowhere until these key issues are addressed. Forcing the differences into the open and educating the public about why such issues matter so much will have its own consequences. This would clearly expose such matters in detail and encourage support for the school board's position that schools need the best teachers.

Third, one of the broader lessons I have learned and wish to pass along is that I believe an overwhelming majority of Americans appear to support the kinds of changes discussed in this book. The most common reason is that they want what is best for their children. And when schools operate outside of this mission, putting teachers' rights above students' rights, most people conclude that the system is broken and in need of repair. Ockham's razor is alive and well.

But if parents and taxpayers just keep throwing up their hands and lamenting the fixable failures in our schools, nothing will change. We may well be at a tipping point. All that is needed is honest and open discussion on these topics in the public square, at school board meetings, among parent organizations and the like. Remember—"vision without action is a dream." We stand at a point in time when action is needed to bring about the vision of significantly improved schools.

Last, I'd like to reinforce the idea that an overwhelming majority of the teachers in classrooms throughout our country are to be commended for the quality and devotion they bring each day to their students and the teaching profession. I have personally worked with countless kind, smart, highly devoted teachers. While talk of improvement must be a constant in any well-intentioned institution, we must never lose sight of the many wonderful and hard-working educators who ply their trade to the best of their abilities every day.

Think about the wonderful teachers in your community today, and the extra mile so many go in making the school experience worthwhile and rewarding for their students. Perhaps it is that second grade teacher who regularly stays after school with struggling students who need special help in a dignified, quiet setting that allows for extra attention. Or perhaps it is the seventh-grade math teacher who works tirelessly in each class, in addition to mentoring and acting as a confidante for newer teachers each day.

In the end, teachers are an integral part of the community in which they work. Far better for teachers and the communities in which they teach to maintain a relationship based on respect and shared concern for all students. Give and take is crucial. There is a saying, "tell me who is running a given organization, class, company, or team and I'll tell you how good this situation is going to be." In every school, quality education begins and ends with the quality of the teachers and administration. Let us celebrate the unique and endearing efforts of our teachers as they heed their calling. Teachers need everyone's support. They certainly deserve it.

Confession Number Ten

I wrote this book out of deep frustration and despair at knowing we did not always have our best available teachers in the classroom because of outdated labor contract language. While I've been blessed to work at schools where the vast majority of teachers are to be admired and applauded, there have always been a select and distinct minority who simply didn't belong in education. If this book contributes in some small way to improving the quality of the education that we deliver to our children, it will have been worth the hundreds of hours it took to produce. Frustration and despair can be great motivators.

Acknowledgments

So many kind and generous people have helped this project at various phases along the way. A hearty thanks to two superintendents, Tim Ryan and Susan Lusi, both of the Portsmouth school system, along with Principal Joseph Amaral and my dear friend and guidance counselor, Jan Williams. Their willingness to thoughtfully fill out a lengthy survey on educational issues and then sit and discuss their answers helped form the basis of some key issues discussed in this book. Students have been well served by these four impressive educators.

Thanks also go out to Ted Nesi of WPRI News for his interview time, and for pointing me in the right direction for further clarity on causes for our state pension crisis. This led to the illuminating work by *Providence Journal* writer, Katherine Greggs, whose investigative reporting has been relied on and respected for decades. Generous thanks extend to Nancy Mayer, former General Treasurer of Rhode Island, for her two interviews and sharing of knowledge regarding pension issues and the unfortunate political climate that has hurt the state. My former student, and summer assistant in 2018, Dan Pantini, deserves much thanks and many accolades for his tireless work organizing citations and bibliographic materials. My oldest son, Matt, for his deep commitment to critical reading and thoughtful editing for the final manuscript. His keen eye to accuracy and details was a blessing.

Deep appreciation is also extended to the three libraries I frequented over the four years it took to complete this work. Thank you to all staff at The Providence Atheneum, Brown University's John Hay Library, and the Barrington Public Library. Their kind helpfulness will be forever remembered.

I had three critical readers who deserve enormous thanks for their honest and candid assessment of my developing manuscript. Janet Hayden-Jagger gave me feedback demonstrating an exceptional level of loyalty and support. At her suggestion, and with sound reasoning, I deleted an entire chapter which, in retrospect, was absolutely the right thing to do. Jan Williams, my long-time friend and colleague, posed smart, sharp commentary that forced me to include perspectives I had not considered. Her enthusiasm and encouragement to complete this work greatly motivated me. And her witty sense of humor, along with a dry and articulate delivery, were always welcomed. Last among these three kind readers was my loyal and inspiring friend, Chris Ramsden. Rammer, as he is known among his best friends, has an intellect and work ethic that knows no boundary. Honestly. His unfailing support and good council on so many topics during this project were a blessing. Rammer is the kind of man who harpoons an 800-pound giant bluefin tuna and reads Cicero in the same day. Really.

Michael Costello, another confidante and friend, greatly assisted me with technical aspects of the teacher pension issues. His expertise in the financial world, and willingness to discuss and advise me on that challenging chapter were much appreciated.

Randy Edgar, my editor, proved to be a godsend. His keen eye toward enhancing the manuscript, along with his kind countenance made him an indispensable ally. Randy's unwavering concern for maintaining the integrity of my own voice in the book, while using a variety of other sources, helped greatly to preserve an authentic tone. His loyalty and professionalism will never be forgotten.

Finally, my wife, Maria, and children Matt, Kate and Andy have been strong supporters from the beginning. Each has provided their own thoughtful element of guidance at various times throughout this project. I am blessed to have them in my life.

Source Notes

INTRODUCTION

"Education then, beyond all": Horace Mann. See Website citations below.

"Excellence flows from many": Russell Hulse, *The Most Important Thing I Know*, Compiled by LorneA. Adrain, (Kansas City: Cader Books, 1997), 71.

CHAPTER 1

"A hundred years from" Forest Witchcraft. See Website citations below.

CHAPTER 2

"We ought to esteem": Plato. See Website citations below.

"Education depends on the": Louis L'Amour, *Education of a Wandering Man* (New York: Bantam Books, 1989), 4.

"For roughly the last": Evan Thomas and Pat Wingert, "Why We Must Fire Bad Teachers" *Newsweek* March 5,2010, 25.

CHAPTER 3

"Above all, it is expected": Judge Samuel Phillips, The Constitution of Phillips Academy, In Andover (1828), 10.

"Every idea in their". James M. Banner, Jr. and Harold C. Cannon, *The Elements of Teaching* (New Haven: Yale University Press, 1997), ix.

"While pedagogical expertise" and: Ibid., 3.

"Children Learn What They Live": Dorothy Law Nolte and Rachel Harris, Children Leam What They Live: Parenting to Inspire Values (New York: Workman Publishing Co., Inc., 1998), vi.

$20 trillion: US Government Accounting Office, year ending 2017.

"It is a teacher's": James M. Banner, Jr. and Harold C. Cannon, *The Elements of Teaching* (New Haven: Yale University Press, 1997), 11.

"Compassion requires that teachers". Ibid., 85.

"The Teacher": Elizabeth Silance Ballard, *Home Life* Magazine, 1976.

"Authority has the unusual": James M. Banner, Jr. and Harold C. Cannon, *The Elements of Teaching* (New Haven: Yale University Press, 1997), 21.

"climate for serious learning": Ibid., 24.

"mastery of subject": Ibid., 25.

"He carried himself": David McCullough, *1776* (New York: Simon & Schuster, 2005), 42-43.

"A teacher ought to be": David McCullough, *John Adams* (New York: Simon & Schuster, 2001), 38.

"Popularity is not authority". James M. Banner, Jr. and Harold C. Cannon, *The Elements of Teaching* (New Haven; Yale University Press, 1997), 27.

"From self-knowledge": James Kerr, *Legacy: What the All Blacks Can Teach Us About the Business of Life* (London: Constable, 2013), 8.

"Ought to accept their": James M. Banner, Jr. and Haroid C. Cannon, *The Elements of Teaching* (New Haven: Yale University Press, 1997), 111.

"Teachers are ethical": Ibid., 5.

"Discipline is therefore": Ibid., 53.

"Order arises from": Ibid., 55.

"When Elizabeth Shaw wrote": David McCullough, *John Adams* (New York: Simon & Schuster, 2001), 365.

CHAPTER 4

$58,950.00: National Education Association, Estimates of School Statistics, selected years, 1969-70 through 2016-17.

$38,617: National Education Association, Average Starting Teacher Salaries by State. December 2017.

"Teacher pay should be": Robert Moranto, Pay Teachers More-but Make Sure They Earn it. *Wall Street Journal*, May 21, 2018.

"A Union for Professionals": American Federation of Teachers, Mission. July 18, 2018.

"Great Public Schools for Every Student". National Education Association, NEA's Vision, Mission, and Values. July 18, 2018.

"Tenure originated in the": *The Week* Staff, "Taking Aim at Tenure," *The Week*, March 11, 2011,15.

"As teachers unions gained"; Ibid., 5.

"hundreds of thousands". Jay Ambrose, "Across America, workers win rights," *The Providence Journal*, March 14, 2015.

"In no other socially significant": Evan Thomas and Pat Wingert, "Why We Must Fire Bad Teachers," *Newsweek*, March 15, 201

"In New York, Chicago". *The Week* Staff, "Taking Aim at Tenure," *The Week*, March 11, 2011, 15.

"We need to identify". Antonio Villaragosa, "Why Are Teachers Unions so Opposed to Change?" *The Wall Street Journal*, July 20, 2014.

"The Key to Saving American Education": Evan Thomas and Pat Wingert, "Why We Must Fire Bad Teachers," *Newsweek*, March 15, 2015.

"Joel Klein, former chancellor": Jay Ambrose, "Across America, workers win rights," *The Providence Journal*, March 14, 2015.

"In almost every state": *The Week* Staff, "Taking Aim at Tenure," *The Week*, 11 March 2011, 15.

"We ended up firing: Ibid, 15.

"This Teacher of the Year". Mary Ellen Flannery, "I thought I'd stay forever," *NEA Today*, August September 2010, 27-29.

"That in tough economic times": Randi Weingarten, "Students Join Battle to Curb Teacher Tenure." *The Wall Street Journal*, February 15, 2014.

"Keeping great educators". Mary Ellen Flannery, "I thought I'd stay forever," *NEA Today*, August/September 2010, 27.

"research shows that kids": Evan Thomas and Pat Wingert, "Why We Must Fire Bad Teachers," *Newsweek*, 15 March 2015, 25.

CHAPTER 5

Erika Sanzi, "Teachers Unions need to change," *The Providence Journal*, July 1, 2018, A19.

Francis J. Flynn, "No need to change teacher seniority," *The Providence Journal*, July 2, 2018, A11.

CHAPTER 6

"sprang out of the noblest". Katherine Gregg, "SET FOR LIFE-SPECIAL DEALS How the state took care of its own." *The Providence Journal*, March 31, 1991.

"special retirement bills": Ibid.

"one-person retirement deals". Katherine Katherine, "SET FOR LIFE-THE SECRECY Assembly takes care of its own. Of 202 bills for individuals in 1990, ex-legislator was lone winner." *The Providence Journal*, April 2, 1991.

"decade-long binge of generosity." Katherine Gregg, "SET FOR LIFE-Paying the tab. Pensions may be the state's next time bomb." *The Providence Journal*, April 1, 1991.

"in more than 400 instances." Gregg, March 31, 1991.

"ignored arguments about." Ibid.

"one-of-a-kind.' Ibid.

"a maddening chronicle": Ted Nesi, Dec. 19, 2012, accessed Dec. 12, 2017, http://wpri.com/blog/2012/12/19/how-lawmakers-union-leaders-jeopardized-the-ri-pension-fund/.

"annual benefits paid out." Ibid.

"rom $42 million in." Ibid.

"a shortfall pegged at". Ibid.

"retired state workers and": Ibid.

"some union officials voiced": Ibid.

"Officials said they weren't": Ibid

"weren't worried because they." Ibid.

"concerned." Gregg, April 1, 1991.

"roughly 1,190 retirement bills": Gregg, March 31, 1991.

"introduced to make special": Ibid.

"J. Troy Earhart, Commissioner". Ibid.

"with another pension of". Ibid.

"potential $76,263": Ibid.

"had already worked for": Ibid.

"make a one-time". Ibid.

"Former University of Rhode Island": Ibid.

"Everybody was getting money": Ibid

"the change was short-lived": Ted Nesi, Dec. 19 2012.

"DeAngelis had a good". Ibid.

"DeAngelis said he got": Katherine Gregg, "Pension fund cuts possible," *The Providence Journal*, June 13, 1990.

the second year in" Ted Nesi, Dec. 19, 1991.

"once-a-year objection": Gregg, March 31, 1991.

"these bills are against": Ibid.

"How unbelievably bad" the state's: Nancy Mayer, interview by Michael Marra, August 6, 2018.

"No ulterior motives": Nancy Mayer, interview by Michael Marra, August 16, 2018.

"Re-election was never a concern": Nancy Mayer, August 6.

"It's kind of fun": Nancy Mayer, August 16, 2018.

"I had a fiduciary". Nancy Mayer, August 6, 2018.

"local, state and federal": Bob Bryan, "The US government has a $20.4 trillion retirement problem," *Business Insider*, April 6, 2016, accessed August, 2018, https://www.businessinsider.com/us-government-7-trillion-pension-shortfall-2016-4.

"Any proposed reform": Gina Raimondo, *Truth in Numbers: The Security and Sustainability of Rhode Island's Retirement System*, Office of the General Treasurer, June 2011, 2.

"immediate and direct consequences". Ibid.

"The problem does not". Ibid.

"a poorly designed system": Ibid.

"the hardworking Rhode Islanders": Ibid.

"if the state has": Ibid.

"sound actuarial practices": Ibid.

"key decisions". Ibid.

"had the effect of". Ibid.

"as early as 1974": Ibid.

"Continuously monitoring actuarial deficits". Ibid.

"unrealistically optimistic assumptions": Ibid.

"generous benefit improvements without": Ibid.

"from age 60 and/or": Ibid.

"the amount required to": Ibid, 5.

"routinely earn retirement benefits": Ibid, 4.

"the true normal cost". Ibid, 5.

"With retirees living longer". Ibid.

"Investment returns failed to": ibid.

"just under 6.5 percent": S&P 500 Return Calculator, with Dividend Reinvestment, DQYDJ, August 10, 2018,

"he was a man". Marcus Aurelius, *Meditations*, (New York: The Modern Library, 2003),

CHAPTER 7

"a person or situation": Louis L'Amour, *Education of a Wandering Man*, (New York: Bantam Books, 1989), 76.

"You miss one hundred": Wayne Gretsky. See Website citations below.

CHAPTER 8

"There are two ways:" Edith Wharton. See Website citations below.

"every child deserves effective": *National Council on Teacher Quality*, Erica E. Phillips,

"Teacher Tenure Put to the Test in California Lawsuit," *The Wall Street Journal*, Feb. 14, 2014.

Figure 8.1 ("Seniority Factor"): Ibid.

"The council points to": Ibid.

"a culture of asking". James Kerr, *Legacy*, (London: Constable, 2013), 15.

"value-based and purpose-driven": Ibid, 13.

"Vision without action is": Ibid, 11-12.

CHAPTER 9

"Education should provide the": Louis L'Amour, *The Education of a Wandering Man*, (New York. Bantam Books, 1989), 3.

BIBLIOGRAPHY

Aurelius, Marcus. Meditations. New York: The Common Library, 2003

Banner, James M. Jr., and Harold C. Cannon. *The Elements of Teaching*. New Haven: Yale University Press, 1997.

BrainyQuotes.com, BrainyMedia Inc. 2019. www.brainyquote.com/quotes /horace_man-137201, accessed February 19,2019

Glasser, William. *The Quality School Teacher*. New York: HarperCollins, 1993.

Kerr, James. *Legacy: What the All Blacks Can Teach Us About the Business of Life*. London: Constable, 2013.

Kozol, Jonathan. *Savage Inequalities*. New York: Crown Publishers, 1991.

Levine, Madeline. *The Price of Privilege*. New York, HarperCollins, 2006.

L'Amour, Louis. *Education of a Wandering Man*. New York: Bantam Books, 1989.

McCullough, David. *1776*. New York: Simon & Schuster, 2005.

McCullough, David. *John Adams*. New York: Simon & Schuster, 2001.

McCullough, David. Truman. New York: Simon & Schuster, 1992.

Shaara, Michael. The Killer Angels. New York: Ballantine Books, 1974.

Sizer, Theodore R., and Nancy Faust Sizer. The Students are Watching. Boston: Beacon Press, 1999.

Websites

BrainyQuotes.com, BrainyMedia Inc., accessed February 19,2019. Quotes taken from Brainy-Quotes.com include: Horace Mann, page 2, Dr. Forest e. Witcraft, page 5, Plato, page 9, Leo Buscaglia, 50, Margaret Mead, page 61, Wendy Kopp 72, Edith Wharton, page 83, Ma Jaya Sati Bhagavati, 97.